Beyond GUILT AND POWERLESSNESS

Y0-EGH-609

George S. Johnson

Augsburg Fortress

Minneapolis

BEYOND GUILT AND POWERLESSNESS: Christian Response to Human Suffering

Published under the auspices of the hunger program and studies departments of the Commission for Church in Society of the Evangelical Lutheran Church in America

1   2   3   4   5   6   7   8   9   0   1   2   3   4   5   6   7   8   9

CONTENTS

Acknowledgments and gratitude

I want to thank Gene Sylvestre and Hal Dragseth who served with me on a steering committee that guided this project to its completion; to John L. Halvorson whose support has kept the concept and work a live option; to Kristin Paulson for typing the manuscript into the computer; to Bill Kirlin-Hackett and Milo Thornberry for helpful critique and suggestions; and to the many people who responded to the invitation to contribute stories of their experiences. I am sorry we couldn't include all of them in this volume.

● ● ●

I dedicate this work with deep appreciation to C. Dean Freudenberger, professor of international studies at the School of Theology in Claremont, California, who first helped to raise my consciousness about global justice and ecological issues; and to my wife, Vivian Elaine, whose love, patience, and partnership have encouraged me to continue my calling.

Preface

This book of meditations allows us to hear the voices of many who are moving from believing in Jesus to following him. Dag Hammerskjold, Dietrich Bonhoeffer, Teilhard de Chardin, Carter Heyward, Bonnie Jensen, Walter Brueggemann, Elias Chacour, Evelyn Eaton Whitehead, the author himself, George S. Johnson, and others, give us glimpses into their struggles to be faithful disciples of Jesus and invite us to enter into the joy and sorrow of this struggle with them.

Perhaps the unique and moving feature of this book, however, is the voices of regular "pew-sitting" Christians who are not known beyond their family, congregation, and community but who speak eloquently through the pages of this book about what discipleship means to them.

This book stimulates the mind and motivates the will, but it also moves the heart. It calls us to experience celebration, outrage, conversion, sorrow, joy, suffering, pain, hope, fear, and community. The author is not afraid to direct our gaze at the bloated bellies of starving children or the poignant pain of Palestinian refugees kept 40 years from their homes. He leads us into the darkness within us and around us. Yet, the result is not despair, debilitating guilt, or a sense of powerlessness, but an experience of pathos and solidarity that purges, moves, and motivates.

Reading this collection of the sayings of contemporary "saints" will enrich us by allowing us to share in their lives and faith and to gain from them new insights into who the biblical God is and how this God works to create shalom on the earth. It may also make the reader more aware of God's call to us to join in this work. I recommend this book highly as devotional reading for Lent or Advent or any other time of the year.

Jerry L. Folk, executive director
ELCA Commission for Church in Society

INTRODUCTION

● ● ●

This booklet is about hope—hope that energizes. Its purpose is to encourage people who want to move beyond feelings of guilt and powerlessness in their response to the widespread and growing suffering of people, as well as to our environment. It is written with the conviction that God's people are called to believe that things can be different, and that with our God we are not powerless. God is not powerless.

There is a growing sense of frustration and apathy toward long-range social responsibility. During my 15 years of involvement with the issues of hunger and poverty (seven as director of the hunger program of the former American Lutheran Church), I came into contact with scores of people who wanted to respond, who wanted to act compassionately toward human suffering, but who felt trapped, confused, and helpless.

Many became involved and active but later were discouraged or lost their sense of urgency. Some sympathized but turned their energies toward something easier to handle. A few became upset and critical out of frustration at not being able to make a difference or see any progress. Others felt personally attacked by approaches that were being used.

Guilt, powerlessness, and fear

The most common causes of this sense of being trapped seem to be guilt, powerlessness, and fear. These are dragons that paralyze the church in its efforts to move beyond a surface kind of charity toward oppressed people. Today the church needs to be liberated from this apathy and fear. We need a fresh outpouring of the Holy Spirit, who empowers people with hope. *Guilt* is ours. We do things that cause disharmony in God's created order. Guilt doesn't cause; we do. Guilt happens because of failure to love our neighbor and because of our apathy toward creative response to human suffering. We express our guilt in many forms.

To avoid feeling guilty about a hungry world, we may stay at surface-level analysis or move to issues that are easier to solve. Or, as one chapter suggests, guilt may be preferred to the pain and uncertainty of solidarity with those who cry for justice. Could it be that while we complain about guilt, we actually prefer it to enlightened analysis and action?

Powerlessness is another dimension to the feeling of frustration. The issues are so complex. Analyses differ. We ask ourselves: "What can I do that will make a significant difference? Whom shall I believe? I've done the letter writing. I've gone to hunger conferences and workshops. I've tried to simplify my life-style. I give generously to hunger causes. I'm tired. Where can I find a better feeling about myself? My energy and motivation are drying up. Given the resulting frustration, why bother?" Such confusion often leads to paralysis and apathy. A sense of defeat and despair plagues the human spirit when it is unable to move beyond powerlessness.

Fear is another hindrance to creative response to human suffering. The statistics are frightening. The future looks grim for all of us if present trends continue. I conclude that to get involved may lead to changes I'm not ready to make. Some of my beliefs and values may be challenged. The systems that have blessed me may be examined and found wanting. My security and prosperity may be jeopardized. I can sleep better at night when I am ignorant of the reality of human suffering and its connection to my acceptable life-style. Who wants to be labeled Communist or subversive? So, because of these types of fears, I keep my distance from the tough questions. I escape into other worthy causes or none at all. Or I may gravitate toward a theology or church that emphasizes "otherworldly" issues.

As missionary Tom Soeldner puts it, "We are all infected by fear that robs us of our humanity and then makes us a cause of fear to others. It is both a fear of things beyond our control and a fear related to our guilt for not doing those godly things that are within our power. Finally, I suspect, it is a fear of a righteous God, whom we know sees our failures and our self-centeredness. In the face of this God we attempt to justify ourselves to prove our worth, even our superiority. In the process we only manage to convict ourselves anew and increase the burden of our guilt and fear."

While I have encountered many people who felt trapped by guilt, powerlessness, and fear, I also have had the privilege of knowing many others who, for one reason or another, were able to move beyond these frustrations and continue steadfast in the struggle. They are an inspiration to all of us. Knowing that their experiences could be an encouragement to others, I have asked permission to include some of their stories and discoveries in this resource.

Stages in the journey

We are at different stages in our journey of faith and social responsibility. The journey is not always straight or forward. Sometimes we go back and forth or up and down. Progress may not always be measurable or visible. This should not discourage us, since the apostle Paul reminds us that "now we see in a mirror dimly . . . now [we] know in part." The important thing is not to give up or accept easy escape routes. Again Paul's words encourage us; "Let us not grow weary in well-doing, for in due season you shall reap, if we do not lose heart."

The chapter titles do not mean to suggest that everyone moves from one particular experience to the other if they are responsible Christians. It may be that you will move back and forth, for example, from certainty to ambiguity and from ambiguity to certainty (see Chapter 12). You may not identify with some of the stories or struggles suggested in these chapters. Pick and choose what to read, depending on the place in which you find yourself at a given time. Be ready to come back another time. Have patience and the willingness to be influenced or nudged by the Spirit. God accepts you where you are but never wants to leave you the same.

Awaken, encourage, and challenge

This booklet is meant to be a resource for the purpose of reflection, encouragement, challenge, and action. The energy with which you respond may come from someone else's experience or from an unexpected spin-off. The stories, quotations, verses, prayers, questions, and pieces of art are intended to awaken thought, spark imagination, and precipitate action. The chapters are not arranged in any permanent order or design. Certainly they do not exhaust the list of experiences we have as we move beyond guilt and powerlessness.

You may recognize yourself in many of these stories. You will meet the Word in the words and be apprehended, exposed, summoned, and empowered. It is good to wrestle with God and not let go until we are blessed, knowing that God won't let go of us. Sometimes the encounter with God questions us more than it answers our questions. We often are taken by surprise, asked to accept paradox, or caught up in mystery. Remember the Spirit is like the wind. It blows where it wills and you know not from whence it comes or where it goes. You may not be able to explain what's happening to you.

As you read you are invited to allow your imagination to carry your thoughts beyond the words on the page into the personal arena of your experiences and conversations with God. Take time to reflect on the questions raised for you. Allow feelings to surface. Learn to ponder. Feel free to pick up this resource for short periods of devotion or brooding. Share the experience you are having with others. Add your story to these as you move beyond the stalemate or valley you may be in. May God bless your imagination and give you courage to act on behalf of others.

2 CORINTHIANS 4:7–10, 16

But we have this treasure in earthen vessels, to show that the transcendent power belongs to God and not to us. We are afflicted in every way, but not crushed; perplexed, but not driven to despair; persecuted, but not forsaken; struck down, but not destroyed; always carrying in the body the death of Jesus, so that the life of Jesus may also be manifested in our bodies. . . . So we do not lose heart."

George S. Johnson
Circle Pines, Minn.
March 1989

FROM STRUGGLE
TO CELEBRATION

It is a matter of doing justice, of standing up to be counted, a stand infused by the passion of the Holy Spirit; informed by wise perception of the wholeness, the breadth, the interdependence of the issues at hand; and empowered by prayer. Without prayer, passion may become restless, manic activity. Without prayer, wisdom is empty and becomes mere intellectualizing, the spinning of conceptual wheels to no particular end. Without prayer, for example, theology may be about God, but seldom draws us farther into God. Without prayer, justice is doomed to disillusionment because we are unable to see beyond what they can see and all we see is injustice.

Carter Heyward

People who have not learned to celebrate in the midst of struggle soon burn out or become cynical and negative. Sometimes they quit and find a new cause to join. Without times of singing and celebration in our lives, we are no longer fun to live with; we end up alienating people rather than drawing them into our circle of friends and supporters.

Those who constantly struggle to survive in Third-World situations find ways to celebrate. Music and dance are often used to lift their spirits and give cause to enjoy one another. They demonstrate that God has made us to celebrate. They become energized with hope by taking time to celebrate.

We celebrate God's presence and the gift of shared bread when we gather for the Eucharist. We celebrate creation when we take time to enjoy flowers, birds, and our bodies. We celebrate each other when we take time to be with one another in the absence of a business agenda. We celebrate the earth when we eat and enjoy food. We celebrate the image of God within us with healthy humor, creative art forms, a sense of accomplishment, and human touch.

11

Our efforts to alleviate human suffering always will be a struggle. There will be pain and disappointment. The gift of celebration will keep us from despair and distortion. It will send us back into the struggle with renewed vision and hope. Setting aside times to celebrate and pray is an investment in hope.

Christians have set a high priority on gathering together regularly for worship. The center of focus is the *good news,* the gospel. Worship time is celebration time. We need worship forms that release power both within the individual and in the community. In the setting of corporate worship we can lift up the cries of pain as well as the reasons to rejoice, knowing that we are all one body in Christ. In our liturgies and prayers we weep with those who weep and rejoice with those who rejoice.

God's people have learned to celebrate even in the midst of darkness and chaos. In darkness there often is the birthing of something new. Creativity comes from the depths, says Matthew Fox, and part of the depths is our darkness, chaos, and uncertainty. The chaos of Good Friday yielded to the creativity and newness of Easter. Knowing this, we are encouraged to celebrate in the midst of struggle.

● ● ●

A missionary writes

Yesterday I joined in a celebration of the retirement from the South African Council of Churches of Dr. Wolfram Kistner. He is a small, fragile man of immense courage and perseverance, dedicated both to the gospel of Jesus Christ and to the liberation struggle in southern Africa. It was the day after the South African government's latest crackdown on the most effective groups and individuals involved in that struggle. Frank Chikane, the general secretary of the council, was one of those persons who paid tribute to Dr. Kistner.

Frank noted the contrast between such a celebration and the devastating context of the government's action of the previous day. It reminded him, he said, of his time in detention, when he was given food so rotten he could not eat it and told to wash his dishes and himself with the water from the only source in his cell, the toilet. He said that when the prisoners had any time together, they would share such stories and laugh at them, sometimes uncontrollably. Or when they spoke about certain aspects of their torture at the hands of the police, they could laugh at such horrible things, and he told them, "If we could not laugh, we could not survive."

I think that perhaps this laughter is what remains of faith when one has known only the cross and death. People stand here amid the groaning of all creation, as if before Easter: open to its inbreaking, longing for it, but not assuming that they know either its time or its character. They stand here in the community of victims and witnesses, waiting for—what?—waiting for the kingdom of God. What else could there possibly be to answer the victims' anguished impotence? Could it be that this laughter is a mustard seed's worth of faith? Could it be that it is the kingdom already breaking in?

Tom Soeldner

The primary setting in which Israel experienced and celebrated justice was her worship. Worship in Israel was not a setting preoccupied with the other world, or with sacrifices only, which is a distorted picture. No, justice and the advancement of justice and the proclamation of justice was the very function of worship, to mediate God's justice for the world. Worship in Israel, whether it was influenced by the Exodus-Sinai tradition or the David Temple tradition of Jerusalem, had in its center the experience of the gift of God's justice and the proclamation of the justice for the world and for Israel. The psalms document these facts clearly. So do the traditions of the Exodus-Sinai covenant in the Pentateuch and elsewhere, and even the priestly code expresses, through its structure of Leviticus, that worship and social ethos belong together.

Rolf Knierim

EXODUS 24:11
They beheld God, and ate and drank.

ISAIAH 58:6–9

Is not this the fast that I choose: to loose the bonds of wickedness, to undo the thongs of the yoke, to let the oppressed go free, and to break every yoke? Is it not to share your bread with the hungry, and bring the homeless poor into your house; when you see the naked, to cover him, and not to hide yourself from your own flesh? Then shall your light break forth like the dawn, and your healing shall spring up speedily; your righteousness shall go before you, the glory of the Lord shall be your rear guard. Then you shall call, and the Lord will answer; you shall cry, and he will say, 'Here I am.'

REFLECTION • *ACTION*

1. Think of someone you would like to celebrate without waiting for a birthday or holiday. Find a way to let that person know how much you appreciate him or her.

2. Celebration is meant to be done in community. It often is accompanied by eating together. What does this tell us about celebration? Check off on your calendar those planned upcoming celebrations.

3. Think of the different things we celebrate at the Eucharist. How does it empower us for the struggle? Invite someone in pain (that is, someone who is poor) to join you at Holy Communion and/or to have a meal in your home.

4. Read *The Eucharist and Human Liberation* by Tissa Balasuriya, Orbis, 1977, or *The Coming of the Cosmic Christ* by Matthew Fox, Harper & Row, 1988.

● ● ●

FROM BELIEVING
TO FOLLOWING

I don't know who—or what—put the question; I don't know when it was put. I don't even remember answering. But at some moment I did answer yes to someone—or something—and from that hour I was certain that existence is meaningful and that, therefore, my life, in self-surrender, had a goal. From that moment I have known what it means "not to look back," and "to take no thought for the morrow."

Dag Hammarskjöld

When new members are received into our churches, we don't ask them if they have responded to the call to follow Jesus Christ. We ask them about their beliefs. "Do you believe in Jesus?" No new member has questioned me as to what it means to believe. Most find it easy to say they believe in God and in Jesus.

In our Sunday morning service we stand for the Confession of Faith. "We believe in God the Father Almighty . . . in Jesus Christ . . . in the Holy Spirit." Would it make a difference if we stood and said, "I am a follower of Jesus, who laid down his life for me and for my neighbor" or, "I have decided to follow Jesus this coming week in all I say, do, or think"?

Could it be that in our desire to keep the gospel pure and be clear on the giftness of salvation we have failed to extend the call to follow Jesus Christ as it is given in the Scriptures? Have we been too afraid of the role of "decision" on our part? Is not coming to a decision a work of the Spirit also? In saying yes to Jesus is a decisive no also involved, for example, a no to the royal empires of today that call for our primary allegiance?

Jim Wallis, in his book *Call to Conversion,* says that neither evangelicals nor liberals have grasped the meaning of conversion for these times. It is his contention that any conversion (repentance and faith) that is removed from social and political reality is simply not biblical. His book lays out a strong argument for the recovery of conversion emphasis in the church in order for the church to be able to respond to a suffering world.

Such a conversion emphasis necessitates believing and following Jesus. Many people who have moved beyond the trap of guilt and powerlessness talk about their conversion, sometimes their second or third conversion. By this they mean a turnaround in their lives, seeing things from a new perspective. Such conversions do not negate our baptismal covenant but rather awaken us to what Martin Luther calls the daily death and resurrection meaning of our baptism. Every day we answer the call to believe and follow.

● ● ●

Are you following Jesus or believing in Christ?

It began innocently enough—a friend recommending a book, *Christology at the Crossroads,* by Jon Sobrino. The Salvadoran Jesuit blew most of my theological ducks out of the water. He threw a hat down on my Scrabble board and messed up many of my combinations. He forced me to contend for the ground I had claimed. The question that Jon Sobrino put to me I must share with you: Are you following Jesus, or believing in Christ?

Plunge into the Gospels anywhere and you will likely find Jesus asking someone to follow. The verb is *akaloutheo.* It represents a dominant motif. Why, then, do we hear so little about following Jesus in the church today? I've been in, with, and around the church for more than 50 years, and no one has ever asked me, "Are you following Jesus?" Not when I was in the communicants' class; not when I joined the church; not when I became a candidate for the ministry; not when I was ordained; and never in any of my services of installation. Always the questions have dealt with belief: Do you believe in God—Father, Son, and Spirit? Do you *believe* in the veracity of the Scriptures and the Westminster Confession? Do you believe in the unity and purity of the church?

It is as though we held the notion that following Jesus

was "in" until the crucifixion and went out with the resurrection—that we can take up with Jesus on easier terms on the other side of Easter.

Do you *believe* in Christ? It isn't so hard to answer that. What is wanted is an affirmative response to treasured propositions about the second person of the Trinity. But when someone asks, "Are you following Jesus?" this can get to be expensive. This question has to do with my life-style, my attitudes, my values, my surrender.

If I'm following Jesus, why am I such a good insurance risk? If I'm following Jesus, why, when I have done my giving, have I so much left over for myself? If I'm following Jesus, why do my closets bulge when so many are unclothed? If I'm following Jesus, why do I have so many friends among the affluent and so few among the poor? If I'm following Jesus, why do I have so much privacy in a world that is starved for love? If I'm following Jesus, why am I tempted to overeat in a world where so many beg for bread? If I'm following Jesus, why am I getting on so well in a world that marked him out for death?

Are you following Jesus or believing in Christ? Unfair you say: The two are inseparable. Theoretically, yes, but pragmatically, no. We separate them all the time. If we must err, let us err on the side of following. For one can believe without following, but one can not follow without believing.

Ernest T. Campbell

We Lutherans have gathered like eagles round the carcass of cheap grace, and there we have drunk of the poison that has killed the life of following Christ. . . . We have given away the Word and sacraments wholesale; we baptized, confirmed, and absolved a whole nation without asking awkward questions or insisting on strict conditions. Our humanitarian sentiment made us give that which was holy to the scornful and unbelieving. We poured forth unending streams of grace. But the call to follow Jesus was hardly ever heard.

Dietrich Bonhoeffer

P lease don't think I'm a real "fundie." That's not my background at all. For the past 10 or 15 years I've been working to inform, inform, inform and motivate, motivate, motivate and I've come to the conclusion that all the information and motivation goes just so far. My husband and I are in the midst of a very radical change in our ministry and lifestyle. We feel joyful and thankful and pray that we are being more faithful to our Lord. This is only possible because of a spiritual renewal in our lives that is empowering us to change. I feel so strongly that the whole world needs to change, especially the United States. Our external world will never change unless/until our internal/spiritual selves are renewed. That's the starting point.

Deborah Peters

Matthew 16:24-25

Then Jesus told his disciples, "If any man would come after me, let him deny himself and take up his cross and follow me. For whoever would save his life will lose it, and whoever loses his life for my sake will find it."

REFLECTION • *ACTION*

1. Think through the Hammarskjöld quote. Has there ever been a moment when you said "yes"? Have there been any mini- or maxi-conversions in your life?

2. Why is it easier to think about believing in Jesus than to think about following Jesus? How do you understand the difference? The sameness?

3. Share the story of your faith journey with your family or a friend. If there have been any experiences or turning points, tell about them. The exercise of writing them out may be helpful.

4. Read *Call to Conversion* by James Wallis, Harper & Row, San Francisco, 1981.

• • •

FROM SILENCE
TO SPEECH

"In Germany in the 1930s they first came for the Communists and I didn't speak up because I wasn't a Communist. Then they came for the Jews, and I didn't speak up because I wasn't a Jew. Then they came for the trade unionists. Then they came for the Catholics, and I didn't speak up because I was a Protestant. Then they came for me . . . and by that time no one was left to speak up."

Pastor Martin Niemoller

W alter Brueggemann, in his magazine article "Theological Education: Healing the Blind Beggar" *(Christian Century,* April 5–12, 1986), uses the story of blind Bartimaeus in Mark 10:46–52 to demonstrate what he feels theological education should be helping churches to do. He mentions four things: "Theological education that promises healing and liberation (1) must have sociological imagination, (2) must face the fact that a key issue in healing, salvation and liberation is power, (3) must recognize that the first step in gaining power is bringing things to speech, (4) must be unashamedly Christological."

The third point highlights the importance of speech when the blind beggar cries out "Son of David, have mercy on me." He knows it is Messiah time, says Brueggemann, the time when the blind see, the poor have their debts canceled, and beggars become citizens again (Luke 7:22–23).

"We face a crisis of speech in our time. History moves and life is transformed when the powerless get speech. We need therefore, in all our institutions, to be asking: Who has speech? Who does the talking? Who does the decisive speaking?"

Those who are concerned about human suffering are learning to speak out and give voice to the voiceless. It is important to resist the pressures to be silent. The turning point in the Mark narrative is when the blind beggar is able to speak of his pain.

19

3 DISCIPLESHIP AND CELEBRATION

Transforming energy is released and hope is renewed when our silence is broken and when the "little" ones are able to cry out. We move beyond powerlessness when we use our gifts and resources to enable victims to be heard.

● ● ●

We haven't the right to keep silent

A chilling account comes to me from Bangkok: A friend tells me of the fate of the Cambodian refugees whom we had visited shortly before this spring. They are now being moved from camp to camp; everyone wants them out of the way. This human burden is more than we can bear; if only these people would just disappear so that we could sleep in peace again!

In the meantime, hunger continues to ravage the emaciated bodies of starving children, while poverty and wretchedness darken their horizon.

Last February I asked myself the question, Can an entire people die? Now I would formulate it differently: Will we stand by and let them die? We spend billions of dollars on nuclear arms and billions more on cosmetics; we kneel before the sacred shrine of all-holy oil and make fine-sounding speeches for the entertainment and delectation of the peanut gallery in the United Nations. We sink into hypocrisy and indifference. And all the while, in the poor nations, the shadow of poverty lengthens from day to day. And the shadow of fear as well.

I would never have imagined that I should one day feel compelled to vent my rage against the present as I have against the past.

From Paris, a series of images: Starving men and women somewhere in Uganda. Bodies so emaciated that they are almost transparent. Shriveled children expiring in their turn only a few hours later. "You have to shout; you have to raise a cry of outrage," says my friend who sent me the documents.

And so I shout. I bellow. I alert my journalist comrades. I call up senators and high-level functionaries: *We haven't the right to keep silent!* An entire people is stepping down into

20

darkness before our very eyes; if we do nothing to save them, we shall have been accomplices in their deaths!

But—and I am ashamed to say it—people are tired. Tired of fighting for yet another cause. Tired of throwing themselves into yet another struggle. Biafra, Bangladesh, the Congo, Cambodia, and now Uganda: There is a limit to human comprehension! A time comes when people avert their eyes out of an instinct for self-preservation.

Nevertheless, we have no choice. Indifference is a crime. Not to choose is in itself a choice, as Camus said. To do nothing is to let death do everything.

As for myself, I have seen too much in my life to stand by and watch. It may not be in our power to evade our own suffering, but it is within our power to give our suffering some meaning. And it is in combating the suffering of others that we find meaning in our own.

Elie Wiesel

P olitics determines the kind of world you will be born in; the kind of education, health care, and job you eventually get; how you will spend your old age and even how you die. The church must address itself to, and be involved in, anything that affects life as greatly as this.

Rev. Walter S. Taylor

EXODUS 2:23-25

In the course of those many days the king of Egypt died. And the people of Israel groaned under their bondage, and cried out for help, and their cry under bondage came up to God. And God heard their groaning, and God remembered his covenant with Abraham, with Isaac, and with Jacob. And God saw the people of Israel and God knew their condition.

21

REFLECTION • *ACTION*

1. Think about who has speech, who does the talking in your community. How does your congregation or group give voice to the voiceless? Can this be encouraged through worship and liturgy in the church?

2. Think of ways you can help break the silence of those on the margins of society. Choose one group of suffering people on whom to concentrate. Take time to listen and feel their pain.

3. Invite musicians, artists, writers, and teachers to use their gifts to lift up the cry of those whose voices are not being heard. What gift can you use to this end?

4. Read *Hope Within History* by Walter Brueggemann, John Knox Press, 1987.

● ● ●

FROM URGENCY
TO PATIENCE

*Politics is the art of making possible tomorrow what
seems impossible today.*

Edvard Hambro

Most North Americans are in a hurry to get things done.
When something needs fixing we are programmed to find
the solution and get on with living. When we experience a pain,
we usually can take a pill and be done with it. It is not easy for
us to live with pain, unanswered questions, and problems that
are not solved by our technology, wealth, or military might.

When you add to this the urge to see results, the desire for
a sense of accomplishment and progress, you begin to realize
why patience is needed when you give yourself to the cause of
justice and peace in the world. As one of my friends said, "Put
on your walking shoes because its going to be a long journey
and the terrain is often uphill."

Moses and the Israelites were in the wilderness 40 years
before they reached the promised land. It must have seemed like
a long time. Jesus was 40 days and 40 nights in the desert
following his baptism and commissioning by John the Baptist.
Missionary A. E. Gunderson went to West Africa in the early
part of this century, in obedience to Matthew 28:19: "Go . . .
make disciples of all nations." It was 12 years before he had his
first baptism. The story of the saints is a story of patience and
perseverance.

We must be careful, however, to make a distinction between
patience and indifference. Many reports of human suffering are
emergency situations. It might be a crisis of life or death for the
people involved. They cry for help *now*. Each day that goes by
means more and more death and destruction. Urgent action is
needed. Our delay tactics and apathy are not what is meant by
patience. Some of us need to be shaken out of our sleep because
the situation is urgent. There are things we can begin doing
today that will make a difference.

23

For all who would move beyond guilt and powerlessness there needs to be a balance of urgency and patience. We need to act and we need to wait. There is a time for retreat and reflection and a time for picking up the towel and basin for washing feet. We may not see the justice we are working for come about in our lifetime but this will not discourage us. The vision and the promise are enough.

● ● ●

The pathway of peace

When I look at Jewish history in the decades before 1950, I have the impression that the Jews underwent such a pressure of persecution, of oppression, and the worst was the concentration camps. The concentration camps were a result of the real oppression. Once they were stereotyped as just dirty Jews—*Schmutziger Jude*. Who likes to have *schmutz* dirt at home, or in his streets, or in his towns? Everybody would like to get rid of the dirt. And that's what happened in Europe. They wanted to get rid of the dirt and when you opened the concentration camps, we saw that what was there was not dirt but children of God, massacred and slaughtered. Only then did the Western world began to understand that the real dirt was not on the face of the Jew, rather, it was in the mind of Hitler and those who supported his criminal philosophy. I must come to rest with that because one day, because of these massacres of the Jews, I heard my father telling us in upper Galilee in our village, "Children, within a few days, we will receive Jewish soldiers in our village. They might have machine guns but they do not kill. They are just like us—persecuted people. Poor fellows who were lucky enough to escape a devil called Hitler trying to alienate them. And as persecuted brothers, we have to receive them and I ask you to give them your beds to sleep, and we will prepare for them food and accommodation."

Those times I remember very well because we were asked to sleep on the roof of our house. In Galilee you can do it. You can sleep on the roof of your house and you can count the stars in heaven. It's so beautiful. Therefore we were happy that the soldiers came, and we were sleeping in the open. The soldiers came. We received them. We remained together with our new brothers for more than 10 days, after which we were asked very politely, very peacefully, to leave the village for two weeks because of what will become the golden call: "security reasons." They gave us a written promise that within two weeks we shall return to our homes. Therefore we took nothing at all. We even gave the keys to the Jewish officer. We went and lived for two weeks in grottos and under trees in the open, waiting that these two weeks be finished.

They did not come to an end and here we are with 40 years of deportation, of deprivation, waiting for the weeks to end. When we got really despaired of implementing the promise of those whom we considered being our brothers, we were prevented from any kind of violence because our elderly people, like my father, used to continually tell us and he still tells us today: "You have been driven out from your homes with utter violence and extreme trickery. You have to remember your task to return but never use the same methods because the one who used violence once, violence will be used against him. And with violence you can produce something which is called more violence and what we need to solve our problem is rather to conquer not the land of others but the hearts of those frightened people who consider themselves to be our enemies."

This is very important to understand, how we Jews and Palestinians came to that murderous conflict. After two weeks, my father and the elderly people tried to come back to their village. They were forbidden the right to return. They waited one year, two years. They went to the Supreme Court of Justice in Jerusalem. The decision was in their favor but nowadays, as you know in your society and everywhere in any human society, right alone is a dead letter. Right alone can leave you to be crucified and killed and when you are killed as a righteous person, you are a criminal. You are a dirty person, nasty. Maybe in the so-called free world you become a Communist. If you are from those people who lose their village, their country, their homeland, and you try to say, "I

want it back," you are only right, and you are killed. They call
you only terrorists while the others are freedom fighters. It's
very sad. Very sad. So we had only the right, we did not have
the might, and now as an adult, I thank God a million times
that we did not have the might and had the right only.
Because might corrupts very much, and with the might you
can wrong the right and right the wrong. And that's what
happened to us. Although we were frightened. Although we
accepted to share everything with our brothers. Since we
were the mightiless side, we were portrayed as simple
refugees. Nothing else. Nobody asked why are these people
refugees? What have they done to be refugees? Therefore
compassionate, good Christians sent money to help these
poor refugees survive.

Now I know that money is a very harmful help to give to
your brother. Money is very often a kind of conscience
tranquilizer. You know what it's like? Sometimes like many of
our Christian prayers. If you feel sympathy or you are moved
by the story, the experience of any of your brothers, you
hasten to tell him, "I will pray for you." I wish these prayers
would be stopped. I wish nobody would pray for me or for
the Jew because he is moved by our plight and tragedy, and if
anybody wants to pray, it's time that he pray for himself to be
converted, to make enough space in his heart and his life for
one Jew and for one Palestinian. The charity prayer is not a
Christian prayer. And the money "conscience tranquilizer" is
no help given to God.

Father Elias Chacour

One of the greatest evils of the day among those outside
of prison is their sense of futility. Young people say what
good can one person do? What is the sense of our small
effort? They cannot see that we must lay one brick at a time,
take one step at a time. We can be responsible only for the
one action of the present moment. But we can beg for an
increase of love in our hearts that will vitalize and transform

4 DISCIPLESHIP AND CELEBRATION

all our individual actions and know that God will take them and multiply them, as Jesus multiplied the loaves and fishes.

Dorothy Day

HEBREWS 12:1–2

Therefore, since we are surrounded by so great a crowd of witnesses, let us also lay aside every weight, and sin which clings so closely, and let us run with perseverance the race that is set before us, looking to Jesus the pioneer and perfecter of our faith, who for the joy that was set before him endured the cross, despising the shame, and is seated at the right hand of the throne of God.

REFLECTION • *ACTION*

1. What experiences have you had that have taught you patience? What is the difference between patience and apathy?

2. Patience is not the same as acquiescence or giving up or allowing people to walk on us. When does one turn the other cheek and when does one resist evil being done? How does the biblical message help at this point? How does the Christian community help?

3. Get to know someone you feel has exercised great patience in addressing a wrong. Find out what has helped this person balance urgency and patience. This might be done through reading various biographies.

4. Read *Gracias* by Henri Nouwen, Harper & Row, 1983.

● ● ●

FROM WEEPING
TO SINGING

"Only grief permits newness. If God had not grieved when hearing the mocking voice of nations there would have been no healing. If Jeremiah had not cried his way through Chapter 4 and Chapter 8, God would not have had a new word to speak in Chapters 30-31. . . . The very structure of the gospel is an argument that pain felt and articulated in God's heart permits new possibilities in the historical process—the good news concerns God's transformed heart."

Walter Brueggemann

I was on sabbatical from my parish in Long Beach, Calif. At the School of Theology in Claremont I was enrolled in a semester-long class called "World Hunger and Christian Institutional Response." In different ways we were exposed to the reality of needless suffering of people all over the world. One day in class I started to cry. It came out of nowhere. Tears formed in my eyes and I was embarrassed. To avoid being seen in tears, I lifted my textbook to cover my face.

We all have heard stories or seen pictures of starvation and torture that are enough to make us weep. Even those of us who have been taught to hide our emotions surely find it difficult not to shed a tear or two when confronted with some of the hideous things that are happening today to innocent people. Weeping is a human response to suffering, whether mine or someone else's.

It is important to allow ourselves to weep. Weeping and grieving are parts of the redemptive process, the healing process. Jesus wept. Why shouldn't we?

Theologian Walter Brueggemann says that the church has lost its capacity to grieve and thereby is unable to become a liberating force in society. Perhaps our reluctance to look at the bloated bellies and haunting faces of starving children is a sign of this loss. It might be that in our haste to help, we don't sit long enough with those who suffer and weep with them. It was Ezekiel who sat by the river with the outcasts. After that he was empowered to speak a prophetic word.

When we wipe away our tears (not the same as avoiding them) we can be energized for action. We move through and from weeping to singing. Some of the weeping may continue in our songs, such as the laments in the psalms. Singing is such an important part of our response to human suffering because singing and music lifts our spirits. Music is the language of the heart. Many times, when we don't know what to say or how to cope, a song best expresses our faith. Music moves us and empowers us when nothing else can.

It is important to find music and lyrics that fit the occasion. Sometimes an old hymn will do. At other times we yearn for new songs and new liturgies that give us encouragement and hope. We seek words that address the experiences of pain as well as the assurances from God that God is indeed present in the struggle. We need to encourage people with the gift of music that can help us move beyond guilt and powerlessness.

●   ●   ●

We sing Mary's song

Martin Luther sent a letter to Prince John Frederick, Duke of Saxony, introducing his commentary on the Magnificat. Luther said that it is a fine custom to sing the Magnificat at vespers each night. He commended the Magnificat to Prince John Frederick, saying that it "ought to be learned and kept in mind by all who would rule well and be helpful lords."

Each time we sing the Magnificat, we proclaim to each other what sort of God we believe in and especially, as Luther says, how God deals with those of low and high degree. Luther says we sing it for three reasons: (1) to strengthen our faith, (2) to comfort the lowly, and (3) to terrify the mighty. We will look at these reasons in reverse order.

To terrify the mighty. As a group of Lutheran theologians and church leaders, we fit more properly in the category of the mighty than in that of the lowly. Most of us are White, the color of privilege in our hemisphere. We are mostly middle-class, living very comfortable lives, and rich by most comparisons. Most of us are male, another privileged group in our hemisphere. As church leaders and teachers, we are highly educated. We are the intellectually elite. We are employed in positions of respect and leadership.

Some of us fit all these categories of the mighty. All of us fit in most of them. Luther said, "The mightier you are, the more you must fear," when you sing the Magnificat. We fear because we *sing in faith*, believing God does bring down the mighty.

It is risky for the mighty to sing the Magnificat. It might mean moving from the center to the fringes. It might mean leaving theologically proper talk to engage in simple, frank discussions. Or it might mean risking tenured positions in our schools of theology or jobs in the church bureaucracy, as we speak clearly and forthrightly about the implications of our faith. It might mean risking our intellectual credibility as we respect the visions of poor Indians of Guadalupe.

But we take the risk! We sing the Magnificat in faith, knowing that fear can lead us to repentance, and repentance prepares us for the coming reign of God.

To comfort the lowly. We sing to proclaim comfort to the lowly. Each time we sing Mary's song, we are called to believe once again that God has deep regard for the lowly, the hungry, the poor, the little ones.

I was deeply moved by the story of the poor man's vision of the Lady of Guadalupe. I was struck by how lowly, insignificant people have to beg the church to regard them with the esteem with which God regards them. We are not sure whether Mary appeared in a vision to this poor man. Perhaps we have our Protestant doubts. Yet even if we question the vision, the tragic truth remains: The poor and lowly often have to beg the church to proclaim and live out its message of a merciful, compassionate God! Behind the vision's gilded cactus leaves, miraculous roses, and imprinted cloak is the longing for a God who comes, not in the might of military conquest nor in the ecclesiastical forms and evangelism plans of a mighty church, but in simple, compassionate respect and regard for the lowly, the hungry, the women, the poor, the children.

We sing the Magnificat to comfort the lowly. We sing to put ourselves in solidarity with the lowly and those who suffer. We sing in order to bring in the reign and community of our Lord Jesus Christ.

To strengthen our faith. Finally, we sing Mary's song to strengthen our own faith. We keep announcing to one another the sort of God in which we believe: a God who has respect for the Marys of Nazareth, for vulnerable pregnant, unmarried women; a God who rummages through the dump with the hungry; a God who cries when children are killed and women are raped; a God who sees visions with poor farmers and plants roses on their hillsides.

The successful outcome of this conference will be determined not so much by the confirmation of our theological positions as by the faith of the folks who sit around this table, by the kind of God we believe in as we talk together. Luther said that Mary sang the Magnificat on the basis of her experience of being enlightened and instructed by the Holy Spirit. We pray that this meeting might be the schoolroom of the Holy Spirit.

Bonnie Jensen

I wish to see all arts, principally music, in the service of God who gave and created them. Music is a fair and glorious gift of God. I would not for the world forgo my humble share of music. Singers are never sorrowful but are merry and smile through their troubles in song. Music makes people kinder, gentler, more staid and reasonable. I am strongly persuaded that after theology there is no art that can be placed on a level with music; for besides theology, music is the only art capable of affording peace and joy of the heart . . . the devil flees before the sound of music almost as much as before the Word of God."

Martin Luther

Harold Nielsen, 67, leaned on one knee, with tears in his eyes, and tried to explain what he'd seen in Mexico. "The second day in Cuernavaca you wake up at 3 A.M. and start to cry," he said. "You don't have to go to the university to see something is wrong," he said. "You don't have to take formal study."

Henry Bellars

> **ISAIAH 54:1**
>
> *Sing, O barren one, who did not bear; break forth into singing and cry aloud, you who have not been in travail! For the children of the desolate one will be more than the children of her that is married, says the Lord.*

> **PSALM 100:1–2**
>
> *Make a joyful noise to the Lord, all the lands! Serve the Lord with gladness! Come into his presence with singing!*

REFLECTION • *ACTION*

1. Have you experienced grief over injustice and pain inflicted on others? Has it ever caused you to weep? If so, what follows your weeping?

2. Has music helped you in your struggle? If so, how? What songs (music) seem to minister most powerfully to you? Thank someone today who has given a gift of music.

3. Memorize a verse or two of a new hymn during each liturgical season. Sing it on the way to work or school. Sing songs together as table prayers.

4. Look into new ways to incorporate musical focus into your worship life that will communicate how the Christian community feels about present realities and God's promises. See: *The Borning Cry* by John Ylvisaker, Ylvisaker, Inc., Waverly, IA, 1989.

• • •

FROM IGNORANCE
TO DISCOVERY

Discovery is not always a joyful process. It some-times involves struggle, pain, and confusion. The very essence of discovering is embracing the un-known, loving the confusion as well as the certainty. Discovering is not only about creating harmonies; it also means being with the disharmonies. To trust the discovering process is an act of great courage.

Don Christiansen

L ife is filled with moments of learning and discovery. Watch a baby discover its fingers. How fascinating it is to observe the changes that take place when the teenager in your family first discovers the opposite sex. Church members often come alive when the Christian community helps them discover gifts they never thought they had. Discovery can be exhilarating and life-changing. It also can be painful.

Learning about human suffering can be laden with heaviness unless it is experienced from the perspective of a grace-filled Christian community. Then we begin to see that it is *my* sister, *my* brother, who suffers. When one from among my family becomes a victim, I want to know. St. Paul writes "when one member suffers, we all suffer."

Many Christians have found that face-to-face encounters with people who suffer is the best way to discover what the reality is and how we can respond. It can happen while riding a bus to work, when serving food at a soup kitchen, when visiting with a refugee family, or while on a trip to a Third-World country.

A group leader said to those about to embark on a journey into a poverty situation, "Be ready to meet Jesus in the faces of those you encounter." In the debriefing after the trip, one person commented, "God is trying to say something to us today and is saying it through those in poverty. I wonder if we are able to listen?"

Like seeking Jesus in the face of another, listening also is a key to discovery. So many of our biases, stereotypes, and fears are the result of not being with people long enough to listen to them. When people know they have been listened to, they receive a sense of dignity and power. As listeners we also experience a new relationship with those who suffer. We are empowered and healing begins when we have taken time to listen, not just to words spoken, but to feelings, atmosphere, hopes, and circumstances.

●   ●   ●

It started in the milk barn

I had been milking in the barn, thinking about the irony of producing too much milk while people in the world were hungry, when I remembered an invitation in our church bulletin for people interested in representing our conference on a study tour in Cuernavaca, Mexico. The announcement said the purpose was to explore the root causes of world hunger.

God seemed to be urging me to go and so I sent in my name, never dreaming that I would be selected. The reality of poverty, and the faith of those Mexican Christians living in the midst of it, changed my life.

When I returned home, this basically shy person—one whom the teachers in high school urged to participate more in classes—began to speak and even preach sermons in other churches throughout the Lakeshore Conference of the Southern Wisconsin Synod. Even more exciting was to speak to congregations of other denominations and various other groups.

My church has been supportive of my efforts. We have sponsored a hunger meal and a Seder supper on Maundy Thursday. Currently we have an ongoing program of donating one penny per day from each person to the ELCA Hunger Appeal.

Most important, others have caught the vision of ending world hunger. Another person in my 240-baptized-member congregation has served as coordinator of our local interfaith food pantry.

Sometimes when I am in the barn, milking the cows and thus producing even more surplus milk, I have to think and laugh. When I went to Mexico two years ago, I agreed to work on hunger issues for one year. I found I have a lifetime commitment.

Marilyn Borchardt

S ome day, after mastering the wind, the waves, the tides, and gravity, we will harness for God the energies of love. And then, for the second time in the history of the world, we will have discovered fire.

Teilhard de Chardin

MATTHEW 25:37–40

Then the righteous will answer him, "Lord, when did we see thee hungry and feed thee, or thirsty or give thee drink? And when did we see thee a stranger and welcome thee, or naked and clothe thee? And when did we see thee sick or in prison and visit thee?" And the King will answer them, "Truly, I say to you, as you did it to one of the least of these my brethren, you did it to me."

EXODUS 2:11

One day, when Moses had grown up, he went out to his people and looked on their burdens; and he saw an Egyptian beating a Hebrew, one of his people.

REFLECTION • ACTION

1. The word "conscientization" refers to experiencing the reality of human suffering, then making the connection between suffering and its various linkages to other issues and what justice calls for. To be conscientized is to be awakened and be doing something toward human liberation, either for oneself or for others. What discovery experiences have helped to conscientize

you about various kinds of oppression that cause human suffering?

2. Subscribe to a periodical that will keep you in touch with justice discoveries and happenings in the Third World, not often covered in the media. Some suggestions are: *SEEDS*, 222 E. Lake Dr., Decatur, GA 30030; *The New Internationalist*, Box 1143, Lewiston, NY, 14092; *The Other Side*, 300 W. Apsley St., Philadelphia, PA 19144; *Alternatives*, Box 429, 5263 Bouldercrest Rd., Ellenwood, GA 30049; and *Creation*, Box 19216, Oakland, CA 94619.

3. Read *Rediscovering American Values* by Frances Moore Lappe, Ballantine Books, 1989.

● ● ●

FACE-TO-FACE ENCOUNTERS

In our efforts to respond to the needs of poor and hungry people with compassion and integrity, there is no good substitute for face-to-face encounters with the people we wish to help. Avoiding poor people is easy in our culture. Even people who want to reach out may find themselves blocked by fear.

In *Evangelism and the Poor: a Biblical Challenge for the Church*, the authors suggest some ways of meeting poor people and learning about their needs. Pick one or two as your commitment for this next phase of your faith journey.

1. Volunteer to help at a food pantry or soup kitchen two times during the next four weeks. This will include entering into conversation with the recipients.

2. Volunteer (with others) to weatherize the home of a poor family or elderly person(s) and get to know the residents.

3. Volunteer to serve and/or observe at an emergency center for the poor. Examples might include the emergency waiting room at your county hospital, the courthouse where hearings and trials take place, the food-stamp center, or the legal aid office.

4. Visit the unemployment office on two different occasions and enter into dialog with those applying.

5. Volunteer to go with a social worker or police officer two times on visits that will help you understand the struggles of the poor.

6. Spend a night (from 10:00 P.M. until 5:00 A.M.) on the streets of an inner city, to listen, touch, taste, smell, and feel what goes on and how some people of our society live. (This should be done in pairs or as a group.)

7. Go on a mini (weekend) trip to a Third-World situation where face-to-face encounter with the poor is possible.

8. Arrange for two visits with a refugee or displaced family, one in your home, one in their home, to discuss their struggles, culture, values, and signs of hope.

9. Volunteer to spend a night at an emergency shelter or halfway house and listen to the stories of those who need this service.

10. Visit an Indian reservation and arrange for in-depth conversations with Native Americans and those who work with them. If possible, stay overnight.

11. Visit a prison on two different occasions and enter into dialog with inmates, with a special focus on poverty, racism, and societal prejudice.

12. Visit with two farm families who have experienced foreclosure. Seek understanding and give support.

13. Take time to listen to nature and our environment as it cries out for liberation from exploitation. Ask an environmentalist to take you on a trip that will help you better understand what's happening and why.

Ana de Garcia and George S. Johnson

FROM PRIVATE *TO SOCIAL CONSCIENCE*

The Christian life, while intensely personal, is always communal. . . . The privatization of piety is not part of the Christian tradition and it undermines the Christian life. . . . Christian spirituality is, therefore, the spirituality of Christian community. But it is not Christian community lived in isolation from the world.

John deGruchy

One of Cesar Chavez's children was reminiscing about his childhood. Having the leader of the United Farm Workers as his father was not easy for him. There were many things he regretted about the way things were in his family. But one thing he said he always will treasure from his childhood is that his father helped him develop a social conscience.

How many of us have helped our children develop a social conscience? How do you do that? What is a social conscience?

Most of us are bothered by a bad conscience when we personally have committed sins that hurt a neighbor or friend. If I lie to someone or commit adultery, my conscience tells me I have sinned. Conscience is an inner voice that reminds me that a violation has taken place. A person without a conscience is a danger to society.

The trouble is that too often our conscience is trained to be sensitive to individual violations of God's law but not very well trained to be sensitive to social or corporate sins. As a result we are more easily convinced, for example, when we are reminded about behavior toward a spouse than when we are reminded about human rights being denied the poor as a result of corporate, military, or government action.

Individual sins receive far more attention in sermons and Christian literature than do social sins. Our rugged individualism and personal piety may allow us to dismiss ourselves from any corporate guilt or shame. Yet some of the injustices inflicted on people are not attributed to any one person but to a society that has allowed it to happen.

A social conscience is one that is trained to identify with society in accepting responsibility for injustice done to groups of people. It accepts the social and corporate nature of our lives as well as the uniqueness of the individual. It is able to make connections between larger societal problems and personal decisions we make. A social conscience is a part of what we call compassion. It motivates and energizes us to care about groups of people in more than a superficial way. By it we are united with those who suffer and are able to respond more wisely.

● ● ●

All night I tossed and turned

When I was a seminary student we drew numbers in the spring to see who would get first choice of rooms in the dormitory in the fall. I drew a bad number so I came back later, pretending I hadn't drawn a number yet. This time I was much higher in the draft. No one questioned my clever maneuver.

But that night my conscience bothered me so much I couldn't sleep. I had cheated. How could I be a pastor if I would do things like that, I thought. All night I tossed and turned. So the next day I went to the dean and confessed what I had done. It was a relief to be forgiven. During that time in my life my conscience was very sensitive to individual and private sins. It would lead me to confession and reconciliation on a personal level.

I remember going that same week to hear Martin Luther King Jr. He talked about sin of racism. At first he referred only to the bus boycott in Montgomery, Alabama. I thought, how could humans be so inhumane. Then he went on to talk about racism in the North . . . in the city where I lived. He talked about corporate racism and institutional racism. My eyes were opened to the many ways in which prejudice is present in all of us. I began to see the violence of racism.

40

As I rode back to the seminary with my classmates, we discussed the statistics and facts that made us more aware of racism in our own backyard. We realized that we belonged to a society that was just as racist as the people of Montgomery. But that night I didn't lose any sleep because of a bad conscience. I slept like a baby. There was no inner need to confess my sins to anyone. My conscience was not as sensitive to social sins as it was to my individual sins. Since then my conscience has been enlightened. Now I am more apt to be concerned about violations that are corporate and social.

George S. Johnson

ISAIAH 6:4–5
And the foundations of the threshold shook at the voice of him who called, and the house was filled with smoke. And I said: "Woe is me! For I am lost; for I am a man of unclean lips, and I dwell in the midst of a people of unclean lips; for my eyes have seen the King, the Lord of hosts.

REFLECTION • *ACTION*

1. What has helped you develop a social conscience, a sensitivity to the corporate nature and extent of injustice done to people?

2. What can be done to help children develop a social as well as individual conscience? Can public education contribute to this? What can congregations do?

3. Pick a play or movie that helps to raise social justice awareness. Invite a friend to see it with you. Talk to a teacher about how textbooks, curriculum, and global education can help students develop a social conscience.

4. Read *The Politics of Compassion* by Jack Nelson-Pallmeyer. Orbis, 1986, and *Shalom: The Bible's Word for Salvation, Justice, and Peace* by Perry B. Yoder, Faith and Life Press, 1987.

● ● ●

FROM GUILT
TO RESPONSIBILITY

*Too much moroseness and ethical righteousness still
hangs over the best and most critical prophets of
the West. Such moral sadness and depression, even
among critical voices, resembles more and more the
guilt-ridden sermons of the fundamentalists. The
ethical positions vary, but the spirit of cynicism and
patriarchal pessimism is the same. What is missing?
The* Via Positiva. *Joy. Delight. Wonder at the awe
of being, the awe of being alive, the awe of being
part of the great cosmic divine energy in action.
Without eros, love of life, the* Via Positiva, *imagination is stymied and the very purpose for ethical
action—which is the delight of the universe—is
passed over. To pass over eros represents another
instance of leaping into the second article of faith
(redemption) without pausing at the first (creation).*

Matthew Fox

N o feeling is more common to those who learn of the global
atrocities inflicted on the poor and powerless than the feeling of guilt. Almost everyone who learns of the millions dying
of hunger feels guilty about our overabundance and waste. Guilt
can be painful, disturbing, even debilitating. Sometimes we avoid
issues that cause guilt feelings because we fear guilt. On other
occasions this fear leads us to compensate with hyperactivity,
that is, endless doing to avoid feeling. At best, guilt is a motivator,
and like any feeling, it is healthy, given due and appropriate
attention. Left to itself, however, it does little to sustain us in
the long haul.

Perhaps some of us have been too quick to write off guilt
as unhealthy and destructive. If we avoid anything that triggers
our guilt without distinguishing between healthy, normal guilt
and false, destructive guilt, we are ignoring a deeper reality in
creation. Guilt can protect us from irresponsible action.

Two factors are important to consider. First we must learn, as the following article suggests, to distinguish between authentic and inauthentic guilt. Inauthentic guilt focuses on how bad and how powerless we are, rather than on action we can take or behavior we can change. Authentic guilt produces repentance and invites us to make contact with whomever we have hurt. It leads to responsible action.

Feeling healthy, authentic guilt is a gift which prepares us for repentance, forgiveness, and reconciliation. When reports of injustice and exploitation only lead us to avoid or be rid of guilt, we may miss an important word God is saying to us. Many of us have been raised to view guilt negatively, yet its gift is to lead us to positive, creative action, and above all, to responsibility. Even when we convince ourselves that we are not guilty, we remain responsible.

● ● ●

The gift of guilt

Guilt is a uniquely human response; without it we would be less than wholly accountable for our lives. Genuine guilt is an arousal of the heart, an alarm that warns us of a wound for which we are responsible. Such guilt is a gift, a gift that alerts us to an injured relationship—with a friend, with God, with our own best hopes and deepest values. As psychologist Willard Gaylin observes, guilt is the guardian of our goodness.

The challenge for each of us is to learn to distinguish authentic guilt from its pernicious false cousins. In genuine guilt we honor our responsibility for a relationship to which we are committed. This becomes a grace as it alerts us to those concrete actions by which we have injured others or undermined values. Here my sense of guilt—painful as it may be—is the first step on the Christian journey of repentance, forgiveness, and reconciliation. In the daily conversions through which we grow in love and faith, genuine guilt often is our guide.

But though guilt is meant to be a grace that leads to healing, we know that too often it is instead a curse. The painful arousal seems to go awry; this guardian of our goodness becomes a monster that takes up residence to torment us and distract us from reconciliation. This destructive guilt often arises when we allow ourselves to become victims of external pressures and exaggerated ideals. We then feel wretched for not meeting our own expectations (I feel guilty for not being "the perfect spouse"), or those of other people (I blame myself for not achieving the kind of success my parents had hoped for).

False guilt lures us from a focus on what we have done to an absorption with how bad we are. The mood moves from "I have failed here" to "I am a failure." In this maelstrom of defeat, I lose sight of the particular behaviors that I can and should change. I even lose sight of the relationship that I have injured. Increasingly, the focus is on me—my wretchedness, my failure, my pain. When I succumb to the temptation to "entertain" these painful feelings, I give this disruptive mood power over me. The gift of guilt becomes a curse, and reconciliation escapes me.

Initially, most of us are understandably reluctant to share responsibility for the ancient and continuing injustice in human affairs. "I am not personally to blame," we protest, "for poverty or slavery or terrorism." But maturity brings many of us to acknowledge that we belong to and are active members of this wounded and wounding species. We need less and less to deny our involvement in this shared history of sin and guilt. This need not lead us to wallow in a mood of hopelessness and self-pity. The recognition of original guilt can instead bring us to a tolerance that is blessed with patience. And it turns us, as believers, to our God who does not cease to forgive even such a race. This original guilt, too, is a "bad feeling" that is good for us to know.

Guilt becomes a gift only through the development of a mature conscience. Children do not easily distinguish genuine guilt from false; adolescents often are hard pressed to separate conformity to other people's expectations from the pursuit of authentic values. Only the well-seasoned conscience of the mature Christian adult can discern the face and feel of genuine guilt. This guilt is a precious gift; it alerts us to our failings and impels us to seek the healing grace of repentance and reconciliation.

Evelyn Eaton Whitehead
James D. Whitehead

So let's not wallow in our guilt—but let's not ignore it either. There are many things in today's world for us to feel guilty about. Praise God that Christians know what's to be done with guilt and know the power that can change the situations that give birth to it.

Charles Lutz

ISAIAH 1:17–18
Learn to do good; seek justice, correct oppression; defend the fatherless, plead for the widow. "Come now, let us reason together," says the Lord: "though your sins are like scarlet, they shall be as white as snow; though they are red like crimson, they shall become like wool."

REFLECTION · *ACTION*

1. What role has guilt played in the development of a social conscience for you?

2. How can people be helped who avoid honest encounter with the reality of human suffering because they don't want to feel guilty?

3. Find a few like-minded friends with whom you can talk freely about authentic guilt and corporate guilt. Allow your conversation to be part of the healing process. Organize a support group around global justice issues.

4. Read *Praying the Kingdom: Towards a Political Spirituality* by Charles Elliot, Darton, Longman and Todd. London, 1985.

•   •   •

FROM BLAMING
TO ANALYSIS

"Conventional wisdom" focuses on the victims of hunger and always sees them as people lacking something—food and money, of course, but also technology, skills, knowledge (and, in the worst cases, even intelligence). What if, on the contrary, we regarded these millions of poor people as a rich national resource who lack only power, the power to control their own environments and the circumstances of their lives? By upending it, we shall discover that the problem of hunger is not one of technology or organization but of politics; morally, the issue is not charity, but justice.

Susan George

Entering into discussion with people about why there is this or that suffering in the world can be discouraging and confusing. Some people sound so convincing. Then you hear someone else name causes that are entirely different. Who do you believe? Trust? Then you learn that symptoms are different than causes. Does it really make any difference what analysis you work from in responding to the cries of human suffering? Can the average person really understand?

Without appropriate analysis there are some tendencies that, when followed, lead to powerlessness and a continuation of things as they are. It seems natural, for example, to "blame the victim" when tragedy and suffering happens. If only they will change, then things will improve. The problem is "over there." So we send volunteers, aid, researchers, and technicians to work with the victims and their environment. However, careful analysis and testimony of knowledgeable witnesses may teach us that the causes reach out beyond the victims or the country in which they live.

Another tendency is to accept simplistic explanations of something that is very complex. For example, it may be true that overpopulation is causing increased stress on the earth's ability

46

to produce enough food, but it is simplistic to suggest that if we convinced people to have fewer babies there wouldn't be hunger in the world. By checking facts about food surpluses and inadequate distribution we'd see that the simple answers, in this case fewer babies, ultimately is no answer at all. Or, it is often easier to live with natural disaster as the cause than to hear that relationship of power and control among people is more central to the analysis.

We also tend to gravitate toward explanations that favor our position of privilege. If it fits our economic or theological bias we are more apt to sit up and listen. We all have our golden calves, those ideals or idols we have grown up with which may not deserve the worship and uncritical allegiance we give them. In moving from blaming to analysis, we need a willingness to look at how others see the problem, especially those who are the victims.

Analysis requires that we look at economic, political, and social causes behind the never-ending injustices that cause human suffering. When we observe progress and growth, we need to ask: at what cost and to whom has this program been accomplished? People of faith need to look at theological root causes as well. It is easy to blame sin but what is the sin? The Bible seems to suggest that oppression, not laziness, is the main cause of poverty. God's people are called to correct oppression as well as give charity (Isaiah 1:17).

It takes considerable effort to probe behind the images of starving babies, disappearing family farms, polluted rivers and lakes, and homeless people to discover the root causes. To move beyond guilt and powerlessness, it is necessary to move from blaming to analysis, from blaming others to seeing how we all contribute to the process of oppression. Without proper analysis we may end up hurting the very people we want to help.

●　●　●

The Good Samaritan extended

Around the biblical parable of the Good Samaritan, with the addition of three or four commentaries, all of which are aprocryphal, we understand our role not just theologically, but politically as well. It is this parable that Christians in the Philippines use to justify working within the struggle for liberation.

In the pre-political interpretation, the story is simple. There is the victim. A priest passes by. A Levite passes by on the way to worship. The Good Samaritan comes and we are told in the Bible that his heart melted. No theological motive, just compassion. That is how a Christian should love.

The model the Christian is given for loving is the Good Samaritan who helps the victim. But that is in very personal, individual terms. How does it become political? First, how does it become social?

According to the first apocryphal story, the Good Samaritan came week after week and found victim after victim. He said, "Here is a problem. It is no longer an individual problem. This is a social problem. It needs a social response." True to his good nature and his political limitation, he went around to his fellow Samaritans and collected money to set up a Good Samaritan hospital. Because there are very many victims, you need an institutional response to an increasing number of victims.

But it is not quite political yet. It becomes political because, when you put up an institution like a hospital, you have to hire staff. And you have to have staff-development seminars. When you have staff-development seminars, they start analyzing, "Why are there so many victims?"

According to the janitor: "It is simple. Like you ask me: Why is the corridor always wet? It is because someone has failed to turn off the leaking tap." There are many victims because someone is causing those victims. Oh, the robbers! That is the first lesson in politics. Not to see only victims, but to see a robber.

Normally the church sees victims, helps victims. Sees robber and says, "Don't rob again." Robber says, "I have problems. My children need money, they are into drugs." The church can help the victim and help the robber and see that they both need help.

According to the second apocryphal story, one day the Good Samaritan came one hour earlier. Instead of seeing only the victim, he saw the robber robbing the victim. The victim was not yet the victim. He was resisting. The Good Samaritan says, "I still must love: But how do you love? That is the problem."

Why do we look at ourselves as the Good Samaritan? Couldn't we be the victim? Couldn't we be the robber? Why is Christian morality associated with the Good Samaritan? What is the Good Samaritan politically?

The Good Samaritan politically is in the middle, not quite robbing, not quite victim, not yet oppressor, not yet oppressed, not very rich, not very poor either. We are in the middle, where most of us want to believe that we are. Not involved but feeling the need to get involved. Because that is the ethical call to act. Once you see that, the call is to love. To love in a conflict situation is to take sides. Once you take sides, your next dilemma is, How far do you go?

Father Ed de la Torre

For the Bible, oppression is the basic cause of poverty, but I want also to introduce a middle term that sheds some light: despoliation, or theft. In other words, the oppressor steals from the oppressed and impoverishes them. The oppressed are therefore those who have been impoverished, for while the oppressor oppresses the poor because they are poor and powerless, the poor have become poor in the first place because they have been oppressed. The principal motive for oppression is the eagerness to pile up wealth, and this desire is connected with the fact that the oppressor is an idolater.

There is an almost complete absence of the theme of oppression in European and North American biblical theology. But the absence is not surprising, since it is possible to tackle this theme only within an existential situation of oppression.

Elsa Tamez

If, as I believe, a sense of powerlessness lies at the root of poverty and hunger, what does it suggest for all of us who

49

want to do something to end this needless outrage?

First, what we must stop doing:

We must let go of the temptation to berate Americans for their callousness. Self-righteousness never convinced anybody. Besides, I don't believe that most Americans are callous.

We must stop confusing people by implying that more of the same—increased welfare spending alone, for example— will end poverty. Increased social welfare spending is absolutely necessary but it cannot address the needs of those who want to work.

Instead we must strive to understand why people feel powerless and what it takes to address that powerlessness.

Francis Moore Lappé

> PSALM 72:1–4
> *Give the king thy justice, O God, and thy righteousness to the royal son! May he judge thy people with righteousness, and thy poor with justice! Let the mountains bear prosperity for the people, and the hills, in righteousness! May he defend the cause of the poor of the people, give deliverance to the needy and crush the oppressor!*

REFLECTION · *ACTION*

1. Read the newspaper for a week with an eye toward how the media suggests where the blame rests. What analysis do you see taking place?

2. Take one issue of social injustice and plan to probe deeper into analysis for a period of time. Pray for guidance. Share with others what you discover. Look at who makes the decisions and who benefits from those decisions in the long run.

3. Read *World Hunger: Twelve Myths* by Frances Moore Lappé and Joseph Collins, Grove Press, 1986; and *Bible of the Oppressed* by Elsa Tamez, Orbis, 1982.

●   ●   ●

FROM WORDS
TO THE WORD

We are discovering that the Bible says a great deal about the poor. It all seems askew, for while the poor do get a lot of attention in the Bible, the nonpoor get a lot of attention in the church and usually end up running things. One reason for this is that the nonpoor have become the official interpreters of the Scriptures and have managed to take most of the sting out of the passages dealing with the poor.

Robert McAfee Brown

M any of us are so bombarded with words that we despair of reading anything more about the problems of the world. Our mailboxes are full of letters asking us to join this and that cause. Pleas are made for money to help alleviate human suffering. Magazines and newspapers are full of excellent articles that both enlighten and frighten. There is no lack of words to read or voices that cry for help.

There are times when we need to set aside spoken and written words in order to encounter the Word. Not that such words aren't important. But sometimes we reach a saturation point. More information is not what is lacking, but a time to reflect or time to be alone with God, a time of silence, a time to put our inner spirit in order. From our encounters with the Word we are strengthened and better equipped to handle the call for involvement and risk-taking.

There also are times when we need to return to the Word in order to listen to those parts of Scripture that we have neglected or ignored. Our listening is enriched by recalling not only how the Word comes to us but how the Word comes to others. For example, when we listen to the Word as encountered by the poor, we hear new things because of their unique experiences. Such a word is fresh, energizing, and vital to our understanding.

51

In order for us to move beyond guilt and powerlessness we need to search the Scriptures constantly. There we will find a God who listens to the cries of the poor, a promise of forgiveness that frees us from the burden of guilt, a Jesus who came to preach good news to the poor and set the oppressed free. In the Word we find a word of hope that sustains us when death and destruction surround us, and a young church that gave high priority to sharing with those in need. The Scriptures give us clear warnings about idolatry that causes human suffering and oppression. We are invited to participate in the kingdom where swords are beaten into plowshares and weeping is turned into songs of joy.

●   ●   ●

The power monopoly

Peace is the redistribution of power. Any talk about peace that does not face questions of power is unbiblical.

I particularly want to call your attention to the work of Norman Gottwald who, for this sort of business, is the most important Old Testament scholar we have. Gottwald has helped us see that when we open the Bible, we do not find a bunch of innocent nomads dressed in burlap and bathrobes, but what we find is an empire.

In Genesis 12 it says that there wasn't any bread and they went to Egypt to get bread. Now social suspicion leads one to ask: "How come Egypt had so much bread?" **What the Bible knows is that we are born into a world with social monopolies.** And what Israel wants its boys and girls to learn from little on, is that there is something wrong with social monopolies.

Genesis 47 deals with the questions: "How did we get into this mess?" "How did I get into this monopoly where some people have so much and some people don't have anything?" And there it is said: We got into it because our brother, or our alienated brother, Joseph, was a smart guy and he bought up all the land for Pharaoh.

The first year, when the poor people came for the bread, he said: "I'll give you some bread and I'll take your money."

The second year they needed some bread and he said: "I've got your money: I'll take your cattle." (Call that the "means of production.") The third year, when they needed some bread, he said: "I don't think you have any collateral left." So he said, "Why don't we take your land? We'll take your land and your bodies."

And they said, "Take our land and our bodies. We just don't want to starve to death. We will gladly be your slaves!"

And that is how the monopoly got established.

One very telling little footnote in Genesis 47 says that **Pharaoh took all the land except the land of the priests. (Someone has to bless the empire!)**

Exodus starts out saying that we cried out and the Lord saw and the Lord knew and the Lord remembered and the Lord came down and saved—Exodus 2, Exodus 3.

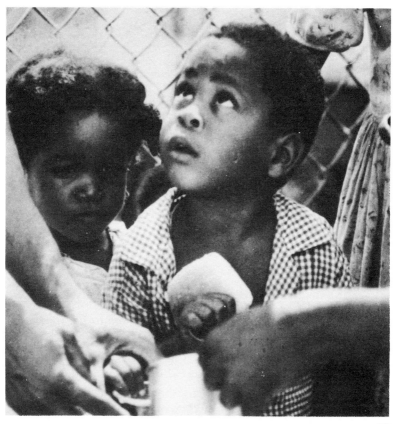

This model of peace believes that the cries of those who are excluded from the monopoly mobilize the power of justice in heaven to rearrange things.

The exodus story is the liturgical reenactment that goes on and on in families and in schools and in business and in the world—the liturgical reenactment of the redistribution of goods and the power and the access.

You know where it ends. It ends in Exodus 15:20–21, where Miriam and her sisters take timbrels and dance. The liturgy invites the community of faith from Exodus 1 to Exodus 15 to start with the cry of oppression and end with the dance of liberation. And the narrative is the enactment of the redistribution of the goods which feels (to the Israelites) like liberation and gift and miracle—but which feels to Egypt and Pharaoh like terrorism and social revolution. *It all depends on where you sit when you read.*

Walter Brueggemann

Biblical passages related to hunger and justice

Genesis 1:29–30	*God gives the world's food to Adam and Eve*
Exodus 3:7–12	*Moses asked to go to Pharaoh*
Exodus 16:1–12	*The manna life-style*
Leviticus 19:9–11	*Leave a portion of your harvest for the poor*
Numbers 11:4–23	*People greedy for meat*
Deut. 14:28–15:11	*A redistribution of wealth and law of tithe*
1 Kings 21:1–20	*Lust for land leads to deceit and oppression*
Psalm 72:1–14	*How to pray for government*
Psalm 82	*Justice to the weak and destitute*
Psalm 146:5–9	*The Lord is just and feeds the hungry*

Proverbs 14:20–21	*Happy are they who are kind to the poor*
Proverbs 19:17	*Who is kind to the poor lends to the Lord*
Proverbs 21:13	*Listen to the cry of the poor*
Isaiah 1:17–18	*Seek justice; correct oppression*
Isaiah 3:13–15	*Why do you grind the face of the poor?*
Isaiah 5:1–7	*I looked for justice but beheld bloodshed*
Isaiah 58:6–12	*Pour yourself out for the hungry*
Jeremiah 22:13–16	*To know the Lord is to do justice*
Ezekiel 16:49	*Sodom destroyed because of neglect of the poor*
Amos 4:1–3	*Elite and wealthy women implicated in injustice*
Amos 5:10–24	*Let justice roll down like waters*
Amos 8:4–7	*The greedy buy the poor for silver*
Micah 6:8	*Do justice, love mercy, walk humbly*
Matthew 5:23–24	*First be reconciled, then offer your gifts*
Matthew 6:25–34	*Seek kingdom of God and justice first*
Matthew 23:23	*You have neglected justice, mercy and faith*
Matthew 25:31–46	*I was hungry and you gave me food*
Mark 8:1–9	*Feeding the multitude, also John 6:1–14*
Luke 1:46–55	*Mary's Magnificat*
Luke 10:25–37	*Good Samaritan*
Luke 14:12–14	*Invite the poor to your dinner*
Luke 16:19–31	*Rich man and Lazarus*
Luke 19:1–10	*Zacchaeus's radical generosity*
John 6:25–35, 47–51	*I am the bread of life*
John 13:1–20	*Jesus washing disciples' feet*
Acts 2:42–47, 4:32–35	*Sharing in the early church*
Acts 6:1–7	*First dispute in church over distribution of food*

55

1 Cor. 11:17–34	*Selfishness in the Christian assembly*
1 Cor. 16:1–2	*Put aside for the needy*
2 Cor. 8:12–15	*A question of equality and abundance*
2 Cor. 9:6–15	*God loves a cheerful giver*
Galatians 2:10	*Remember the poor*
James 2:1–7	*Rich, poor, and God's bias*
James 2:14–17, 26	*Faith without works is dead*
1 John 3:17–18	*Loving in deed, not just in word*
1 John 4:19–21	*Cannot love God without loving neighbor*

LUKE 4:18–19

The Spirit of the Lord is upon me, because he has anointed me to preach good news to the poor. He has sent me to proclaim release to the captives and recovering of sight to the blind, to set at liberty those who are oppressed, to proclaim the acceptable year of the Lord.

REFLECTION • *ACTION*

1. What texts from the Scriptures have been most helpful to you in the empowerment for service on behalf of human suffering? Tell when and how and by whom you were introduced to these texts.

2. Scripture can be used as escape from responsibility as well as for empowerment and comfort. What can be done to avoid using the Bible for escape?

3. Read *Unexpected News: Reading The Bible Through Third World Eyes* by Robert McAfee Brown, the Westminster Press, 1984; and *The Gospel in Solentiname* Vol. I–IV, by Ernesto Cardenal, Orbis, 1982.

● ● ●

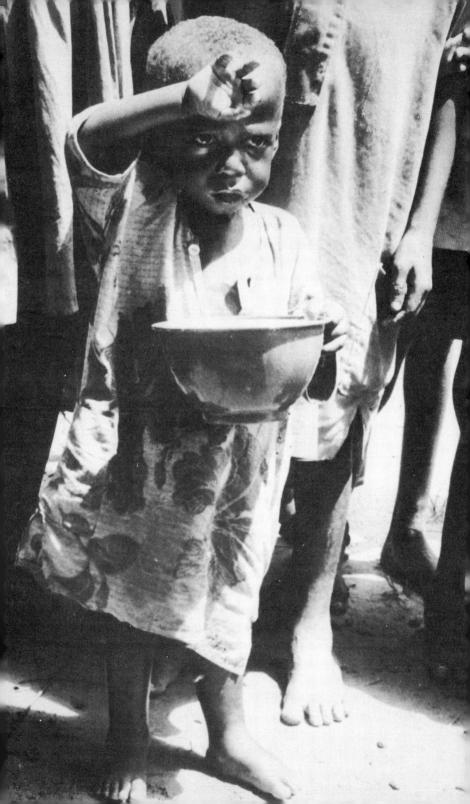

FROM DESPAIR
TO HOPE

*We must become good plowmen. Hope is the pre-
requisite of plowing. What sort of farmer plows the
furrow in the autumn but has no hope for the
spring? So, too, we accomplish nothing without
hope, without a sure inner hope that a new age is
about to dawn. Hope is strength. The energy in the
world is equal to the hope in it. And even if only a
few people share such hope, a power is created
which nothing can hold down—it inevitably spreads
to others.*

Albert Schweitzer

How do you keep going when everything seems hopeless?
Where do you turn to find courage, energy, or motivation
to hang in there when you have every reason to quit? What can
you do about feelings of fear, apathy, despair, and cynicism
especially when it seems that you are all alone in the struggle.

These are questions asked not only by those who are experiencing death and destruction firsthand. They are questions
many of us ask, who live in affluence and among the oppressors.
They are questions raised by people who have joined forces with
those who work to change the systems that perpetuate oppression, racism, and other forms of human suffering. Almost everyone who enters the struggle will, at one time or another, experience frustration, despair, and aloneness.

We can identify with the Israelite living in exile who said,
"How shall we sing the Lord's song in a strange (hostile) land"
(Psalm 137:4)? It is a question asked by millions who find
themselves exiles in their own country, among their traditional
and familiar people and churches. How can we sing of deliv-
erance when every day more of us are imprisoned. When, no
matter who is in office, things don't seem to change?

Hope often is considered subversive by the keepers of the
status quo because it refuses to give up, to believe that things
58

cannot change. Prophets often are silenced or killed because they build a vision of a different world and thereby keep hope alive. Managers of the status quo are enemies of hope. Every center of power in an evil world fears the poet, prophet, and artist because they communicate hope and imagination.

Hope emerges out of the ashes of our dreams because God brings life out of death. What we see is a valley of dry bones, but our new eyesight enables us to see those bones come alive with flesh. The hope of God's people is renewed through the promise of our baptism. It is God's presence we celebrate at the eucharistic meal, and as a result we are energized. As a friend said, "Our hope is deathly foolish, like the cross of Christ." But our foolish hope keeps faith alive and rekindles the fire of love within our hearts. It is this hope that keeps us working toward and expecting the kingdom's coming. It may sound crazy but hope helps us to pray with confidence: "Thy kingdom come, thy will be done on earth."

● ● ●

Letter from South Africa

What hope is there in the midst of the oppression of a police state and the devastation caused by apartheid? What hope, when the situation daily gets worse? What hope, when an entire generation of people has been traumatized and brutalized, when millions of Black children have lived in an environment of fear and violence all their lives. What hope, when further suffering and death is the only prospect?

The hope we have, when we have it at all, emerges out of despair; it is the green shoot that grows out of the oak stump burned to the ground. Our hope is life that springs from death, from a cross. It is that life which flows in people put to death all the day long.

I drove S. to the airport tonight. He is a devoted church worker frequently in hiding from the security branch here. He has been totally consumed by his work for the church and the church's role in the struggle in this land for the past five years at least. I asked him how he keeps going. What hope does he have?

He said, "I think the struggle and all our hopes and dreams for this country were sentenced to death long ago. The flower died—was broken apart—and the seeds scattered. Now all these many seeds, scattered and buried, are coming up in many different places. We are struggling to bring them together. All my work I do because I am a Christian and because I believe that the cross is not only a sign of death but also of hope. The more difficult things become, the more intense the struggle, the nearer suffering and death, the closer I know we are to the new life God promises us."

Great leaders are born of struggle and suffering. So God has raised up out of the South African conflict great Christian leaders, signs of life from the burnt stump. They have names you know well, like Luthuli and Tutu and Naude and Mandela (a committed Christian though he doesn't work within the church), and some names you will never know. Some day we will add S. to those you know.

Tom Soeldner

The compound was first and foremost the children's domain. "Marvelous children of the city of Joy," Kovalski would say. "Little innocent beings nourished on poverty, from whom the life force never ceased to burst forth. Their freedom from care, their zest for life, their magical smiles and dark faces set off by luminous gazes colored the entire world in which they lived with beauty. If the adults here managed to retain some spark of hope, was it not because of them, because of their dazzling freshness, because of the earnestness of their games? Without them the slums would have been nothing but prisons. It was they who managed to turn these places of distress into places of Joy."

Dominique La Pierre

1 PETER 1:3
Blessed be the God and Father of our Lord Jesus Christ! By his great mercy we have been born anew to a living hope through the resurrection of Jesus Christ from the dead.

EXODUS 3:7–8

Then the Lord said, "I have seen the affliction of my people who are in Egypt, and have heard their cry because of their taskmasters; I know their sufferings, and I have come down to deliver them out of the hand of the Egyptians, and to bring them up out of that land to a good and broad land, a land flowing with milk and honey."

REFLECTION • *ACTION*

1. It has been said that people are changed more by exciting their imagination than by reminding them of what is right and wrong. What do you think about this?

2. We keep hope alive by telling the story over and over again. That's why we keep coming back to worship Sunday after Sunday. Find a story of hope in this booklet and tell it to someone you know who may need a word of hope.

3. In what way can hope be considered subversive? To whom is it subversive? Who stands to lose if hope for change is kept alive.

4. Read *Prophetic Imagination,* by Walter Brueggemann, Fortress, 1978, and *We Drink From Our Own Wells* by Gustavo Guitierrez, Orbis/Dove, 1984.

• • •

FROM CERTAINTY
TO AMBIGUITY

When I moved to Latin America I was teaching spirituality and prayer. I had it together on that level and I decided to stay out of anything close to politics or economics. But gradually I realized that I couldn't avoid the political, economic and military . . . mess that is there to be seen. Suddenly I had this image that indeed Christ himself was called political, subversive, and was crucified as a competitor of the worldly king. I remembered that Judas was interested in money, and that money had a lot to do with the suffering of Christ. I realized that there were soldiers and military people all around the Lord, who came to his crucifixion. I saw then that our spiritual call takes place in the midst of ambiguity and ambivalence and that if I waited until I had a very clear, final view of how things really were before I started saying anything, I would never speak. So here I am, a little bit unclear, a little nervous, saying things that I am not competent in, but claiming the competence of the Christian to speak clearly and specifically in a time of crisis.

Henri Nouwen

Most of us are more comfortable with answers than with questions. We prefer closures rather than paradox. There is security with certainty. When faced with a problem we generally approach it with the assumption that information, insight, and proper action will bring satisfactory solutions. We want to fix things right now. In a success-oriented culture, living with ambiguity is not a sign of stability or progress.

However, the reality of a broken world and the variety of analyses of root causes often lead to ambiguity rather than certainty. What we thought, believed, assumed, or followed is suddenly brought into question. It isn't as clear-cut and simple as we were led to believe. Sometimes long-held assumptions are discovered to be inadequate if not false! Receiving more information unsettles us rather than making things clear and easy. Digging deeper only muddles the water.

There usually are two sides to an argument. Listening to the other side is important even though it may be painful. Living, as we do, in a world where everything tends to be labeled right or wrong, we may tend to shy away from ambiguity. Action that is both good and bad is difficult to accept. So people eagerly listen to those who have the easy answers and can assuredly distinguish between the right way and the wrong way.

Ambiguity also is found within us. Part of me wants to lay down my life for those who suffer. Part of me doesn't. Sometimes I may be enthused, energetic, and highly motivated. Within a short time I may feel quite different and wonder why. Which person is the real me?

Wholeness and healing involve pain. Sometimes that includes the pain of ambiguity or the pain of having to change one's previous position. It should not surprise us that our journey into the lives of those who cry for help will be discomforting. We will go back and forth in our analysis and conclusions. In that process it is important to be centered in the gospel, the good news that Jesus accepts us, understands us, and forgives us. It also is important to remember that Jesus' compassion for the poor and the biblical commitment to justice and righteousness is not ambiguous. This can hold us on course as we struggle through the mixed messages we hear and the ambiguous feelings we experience.

●   ●   ●

Journalkeeping in Honduras

Being here, I think, is like watching a terrifying movie. I have seen hideous, nauseating poverty, heard horrifying tales of death, and seen fear trembling across faces. I have met thin and anxious men and women just returned from working in refugee camps who have driven, afraid for their lives, through war on the borders. Honduras shares its borders with El Salvador to the west and Nicaragua to the south. At the United States embassy in Tegucigalpa, I have heard information officers explain our military presence in

Central America as "a good thing." From Hondurans I have
heard opposition to that presence. My life back home is slow,
orderly, and without drama. This trip, like a movie, is fast,
and it keeps breaking with life-and-death events. I am weary,
hot, confused. It has begun to dawn on me, in me, not as fact
but with wrenching feeling, that the lives here are connected
to my life.

Our short stay in Honduras provides us with conflicting
views: the official U. S. position, and that of Hondurans and
international relief workers who oppose our nation's policies.
Most of the members of our group feel great anguish in
muggy Tegucigalpa. We are intelligent, educated church-
goers—"solid American citizens." No matter with whom we
agree, we are discomfitted.

One man in our group, after 10 years service as a soldier
on active duty and as a reservist, felt persuaded by what he
saw and heard in Honduras to resign his captaincy in the U.S.
Army. "I cried for my country in Tegucigalpa," he wrote later
in his hometown paper. "I wept for the hurt and turmoil my
country is creating for millions of Latin Americans. . . . I saw
American soldiers being used as an instrument of a foreign
policy which says, 'If it isn't in the U. S. model, then it is
wrong.' " And whether we agreed or disagreed with this
young man, that morning in the lobby of our hotel in Tegucigalpa, when he told us his decision, we wept with him.

But I will speak, now, only for myself. At this point what
seems most important for the 20 of us from 12 states is not
that we have learned who is "right" and who is "wrong." We
have not. We never will. Few of us will ever even know
"what to do." But our sense of the human family has been
unalterably enlarged. We have seen, many of us for the first
time, what hunger, war, hopelessness, and fear can do. In our
own daily, humdrum lives, it will be difficult to forget the
faces, voices, smells, homes of the countries we visited. We
have also seen signs of hope. Adela and her Base Christian
Communities, Dona Heyde in her CODE offices, the Nicar-
aguan barrios, schools, factories being rebuilt, and people
hoping. When we repeat the Lord's Prayer, the names of the
"our," whose Father he is, have increased. And when we

listen for an answer, we may recall Dona Heyde's statement, that hot afternoon in Tegucigalpa: "God speaks in the voice of the people."

Judith Moore

ROMANS 7:15–21
I do not understand my own actions. For I do not do what I want, but I do the very thing I hate. Now if I do what I do not want, I agree that the law is good. So then it is no longer I that do it, but sin which dwells within me. For I know that nothing good dwells within me, that is, in my flesh. I can will what is right, but I cannot do it. For I do not do the good I want, but the evil I do not want is what I do. Now if I do what I do not want, it is no longer I that do it, but sin which dwells within me.

So I find it to be a law that when I want to do right, evil lies close at hand.

REFLECTION • *ACTION*

1. What questions still go unanswered for you regarding the role of a Christian in responding to injustice and oppression?

2. What has become more clear or less clear, as you have continued on in your Christian faith? As you have responded to the cries of oppression in the world?

3. Think of actions you have taken to alleviate human suffering, even though you didn't have total certainty on the issues. What might God be leading you to do next?

4. Read *Christian Faith and Public Policy* by Arthur Simon, Eerdmans, 1987.

● ● ●

FROM CONCERN
TO OUTRAGE

Our task is to refine the raw ore of emotion and transmute it into the pure metal of competent, systematic—and successful—action. Moral or religious indignation, however necessary, is not enough. Emotion by itself never made anything— no poems, no marriages, no justice. Yet without our untidy welter of love, generosity, anger, fear, outrage, we would never be motivated to change anything; we would be prisoners of the status quo.

Susan George

There is something to be said for diplomacy and tact. We usually make more progress toward improving things by remaining cool, polite, balanced, reasonable, and objective. Being diplomatic is an art we all need to learn and use with discretion.

But there is also something to be said for outrage. Anger is an emotion that can be used creatively for improving things. Jesus expressed strong emotion when he drove the money-changers out of the temple (John 2:13–22). The writers of the Bible are not hesitant to tell us about the anger of God and the wrath of God.

If we are made in the image of God, does this mean we too will be moved to the point of outrage when we witness the injustices done to God's children and the destruction of God's beautiful work of creation? Is it a perversion of love to think that love can be present within us without any sense of outrage toward injustice, in light of global reality today?

Robert McAfee Brown says we need moral outrage within the Christian community in order to bring about the justice of God in society. He claims that we need to recover some of the moral madness of the Old Testament prophets. But that's scary because we've seen how destructive anger can be. We also remember what happened to many of the prophets who spoke out.

Maybe a starting point is to accept the fact that anger is a human feeling that can be a way of moving us to action on behalf of others and that, surprisingly, it is not something foreign to compassion.

I am discovering more and more that if we are willing to learn what's happening to poor people today, as well as to learn the causes of poverty and oppression, if we are willing to get behind and beneath the explanations of poverty given by the beneficiaries from the present systems, we will become more outraged. And that outrage is a sign of the image of God within us. It is part of compassion.

Outrage energizes us for action. It takes us out of our lethargy and indifference. When we are outraged, we look for something to do rather than be content with what may seem hopeless. It takes a dose of outrage at injustice to find the courage to say no to the Caesars of our day who clamor for our allegiance and who want things to remain as they are.

● ● ●

How does one handle the rage in the pit of one's stomach?

For one hour I sat between two volunteer counselors at Black Sash in Johannesburg. I listened as Blacks told their stories of being cheated, exploited, deprived of livelihood, and trapped by unfair laws and regulations. All this was done legally under a system called apartheid. Inside I wanted to scream. How can some human beings do this to other humans? I had to leave before my anger became visible.

Driving through different countries in Africa, I saw fields of fertile land, rich with the capacity to feed everyone. And then I visited the peasants in their poor housing with no sanitation, no clean water, and only enough food to survive if the rains continued.

Perhaps in my rage, in my urge to scream at God, God was screaming at me, at us and at our institutions and social systems that cause and perpetuate hunger and inequality.

I listened to development and government workers tell how aid is often determined not by need as much as by which government follows the directives of our government, or which project strengthens our security and status in the world. Hearing and seeing this made me feel embarrassed, angry, and guilty. Sometimes I cried. I wanted to step up to someone from among those affected by our corporate greed and blindness and say, "I'm really sorry for what we have allowed to happen. Please forgive us."

I asked one of our missionaries, "Do you ever get over the anger you feel when you see how Africans are treated by Whites (both African and non-African), how the poor are left so helpless in their poverty while others get richer?" He said, "No, not really. But you learn how to handle it." Another said, "When you do get over your anger, it's time to leave and go home."

While many of Africa's problems are imported from abroad, many others are not. The rage within also was felt while witnessing the results of senseless brutality and political exploitations by African leaders. One relief worker posed the question to me: "Starve the city dwellers and they riot. Starve the peasants and they die. If you were a politician, which would you choose?"

This feeling of rage in the pit of one's stomach has something to do with God. It is the presence of God in us that yearns for justice and hurts when injustice takes place. Anger is part of compassion. Pity may be void of anger but not compassion. Not until we allow the feeling of anger to surface as we see the injustice and needless suffering of people will we take the necessary action and be able to say, "In the name of Jesus, stand up and walk."

George S. Johnson

Abraham Heschel never "lost the capacity for outrage." During the war years he spoke to a Stanford University ethics class. It turned out that a friend of one of the students, both of whom were Jewish, was producing napalm. The student asked Heschel what she should say to him. "Go to him," Heschel replied, with barely concealed trembling of limb, "and tell him that if he continues making napalm he forfeits the name of Jew. Go to him and tell him that if he continues to create such things he forfeits the name of human being. Go to him and tell him that if he continues to be part of such inhuman destructiveness he sins against creation and the Creator. Go to him and plead with him to repent and ask for mercy while there is still time to do so."

Robert McAfee Brown

AMOS 5:21–24

I hate, I despise your feasts, and I take no delight in your solemn assemblies. Even though you offer me your burnt offerings and cereal offerings, I will not accept them, and the peace offerings of your fatted beasts I will not look upon. Take away from me the noise of your songs; to the melody of your harps I will not listen. But let justice roll down like waters, and righteousness like an everflowing stream.

REFLECTION · *ACTION*

1. Can you think of any one social issue over which you have become outraged—enough to speak out or take some action? Did the issue affect you directly? Or the poor and oppressed around you?

2. What are the social sins of today toward which our moral outrage must be directed? Compare your list with that of a friend. Discuss who benefits if things remain as they are.

3. How can we distinguish between anger and hatred? How can anger be a source of empowerment for change?

4. Read: *Saying Yes and Saying No, on Rendering to God and Caesar,* by Robert McAfee Brown, Westminster, 1986.

•   •   •

FROM GUILT
TO SOLIDARITY

Before I arrived in Namibia I was deeply pained already as an American, pained by what my country, my people, I—do to so many of the people of the world. Many of these people have now become dear friends. I find it painful to think of leaving them and even more painful to think of returning to a land and people who know and think so little about these people, their struggle, and our complicity in the forces that continue to oppress them.

And I wonder: "When I return home, will I remember and will I continue to stand in solidarity?" I think it is much easier to do that here. But I want to clearly stand, live, and act in solidarity. The relationship is not merely some spiritual reality. It is that. There is definitely the Transcendent who operates in our relationships, and is able to pull us out of our own little world to a broader vision and common ground.

We are brothers and sisters in Christ on this earth, sharing common resources. I think until we are able to hear these people and let ourselves be touched by their reality, their pain, and their hunger for an opportunity to live as the whole people God has created them to be—we will not be able to be changed in such a way that we live as sisters and brothers in Christ.

Eva Jensen

In another chapter we looked at the positive side of guilt and the importance of moving from guilt to repentance, forgiveness, reconciliation, and responsibility.

Another analysis of a common response to human suffering uncovers the tendency to prefer guilt to pain, the pain of entering into our neighbor's suffering. It is possible to choose to feel debilitating guilt rather than to become deeply involved in understanding the reality and root causes of suffering. Guilt becomes an escape from a worse pain, the pain of solidarity with the victims of greed and power, the pain of seeking to understand. Guilt may seem easier to live with than going through death and resurrection.

Each week we join the Christian family at worship and confess that we are "by nature sinful and unclean" and wait for the absolution to be announced so that we can get on with our living. Guilt, confession, and the announcement of forgiveness becomes a neat package we receive each Sunday and thereby avoid the agony of living the pain of brokenness and solidarity that leads to healing and wholeness. Guilt of this kind is not only tolerable but falsely secure.

There are times when the word of forgiveness is most needed and there are times when we need to move from guilt to pain in order to become a part of the healing process. Maybe the sermon shouldn't give closure to the issue but should lead us to be open for the Spirit to work. It is painful to have to wrestle with the question. Preaching that always closes with neat remedies and easy answers may not be biblical preaching. It could be part of the problem if it encourages God's people to support the status quo rather than imagine the way things could be different and act accordingly.

Power is found in weakness. Weakness comes from the willingness to experience pain in solidarity with those who suffer. Such pain awakens the need for repentance, our yearning for forgiveness, and our growth in becoming the people of God. It bonds us together with all creation.

Journal notes on a visit with the mothers of the disappeared in El Salvador

In 1981, they took my first son. Then they beat me up. He was taken between 1 and 2 A.M. Soldiers told me if I went further, this is where my body would be forever. He hit me with the butt of his rifle. Later I went to National Police, National Guard—today he is still disappeared. I went to look in cemeteries, ravines, where they throw bodies; one place

there were 32 bodies. I cried. Many other mothers looked.
Another place I found seven bodies beheaded. Another place
I found more bodies without heads. Later I looked another
place and found nine bodies. For three months we looked.
One day my 13-year-old son was taken and shot by a soldier.
He had worked construction—never done anything
subversive. I asked the soldiers, why? They said to claim the
son and not tell anyone. Later in 1981 they took another son
out of our home between 3 and 4 in the morning, and took
him away in a truck. I asked why? It is the only son left. They
said they were not interested. Told me not to talk or I would
disappear. Put blindfold on me—and let me touch my son. I
remember how I loved him. This is why I joined the
Committee of Mothers of the Disappeared. I found him one
day, tortured, shot two times in the head—in the heart—his
head was smashed—ribs broken—his arms bloody. I could
not sleep or eat. I cried. I also have two brothers and one
cousin missing. I ask you to ask your leaders to quit putting
their hands in our country. Salvador is able to plan its own
destiny. Arms are being sent for violence here. We thank you
and send a greeting to mothers in America, so they can be in
solidarity with us.

Ken Peterson

W hen you've talked with the people who are living in
fear and poverty and you've held their children in your
lap and you've ached as you have contemplated their future,
you can't walk away and say "It's none of our business" and
still be faithful to our Lord.

David W. Preus

B onhoeffer, in a poem written during his last months in
prison, distinguishes Christians from non-Christians. It is
not a distinction from God's side—God goes to all in their
need, forgives all, and for all alike, hangs dead. The
distinction is from our side. Christians are those who stand
by God in God's hour of grieving. What makes one a
Christian at all, said Bonhoeffer, is participation in God's
suffering in the secular life, joining the divine agony over the

needy state of the battered creation. The Latins call it
solidarity. Bonhoeffer calls it participation.

Larry L. Rasmussen

JEREMIAH 4:19–20

*My anguish, my anguish! I writhe in pain! Oh,
the walls of my heart! My heart is beating wildly;
I cannot keep silent; for I hear the sound of the
trumpet, the alarm of war. Disaster follows hard
on disaster, the whole land is laid waste.
Suddenly my tents are destroyed, my curtains in
a moment.*

GALATIANS 6:2

*Bear one another's burdens, and so fulfill the law
of Christ.*

REFLECTION • *ACTION*

1. Think of times when you appreciated the ministry of someone
entering into your pain. How did it feel?

2. What are some of the factors in modern society that make
it difficult to enter into another's pain? What are some ways
people use to disguise their pain? What are things we do to
avoid seeing pain?

3. Take your child, your spouse, or a friend and go sit with
someone who is in pain. Enter into their pain. See "Face-to-Face
Encounters," page 37.

4. Read *City of Joy* by Dominique La Pierre, Warner Books,
1986; and *A Dry White Season* by André Brink, Penguin Books,
1979.

● ● ●

FROM CONFORMITY
TO RISK-TAKING

O God, make me discontent with things the way they are in the world, and in my own life. Teach me how to blush again, for the tawdry deals, the arrogant-but-courteous prejudice, the snickers, the leers, the good food and drink which make me too weary to repent, the flattery given and received, my willing use of rights and privileges other people are unfairly denied. Make me notice the stains when people get spilled on. Make me care about the slum child downtown, the misfit at work, the people crammed into the mental hospital, the men, women, and youth behind bars. Jar my complacence; expose my excuses; get me involved in the life of my city, and give me integrity once more.

Robert Raines

When the apostle Paul said, "Don't be conformed to this world" (Rom. 12:1), I wonder if he knew how difficult that would be in our day. Did he have the pressures to conform (fear of unemployment, payments due, advertising, and so on) that we do? J. B. Philips's translation of that passage makes it even more vivid, "Don't let this world squeeze you into its mold . . . but be transformed." The pressures to conform are legion and powerful.

Not all conformity is bad. We are safer if we all drive on the right side of the road. It is good that most of us set aside Sunday as a day of rest and worship. But where do we draw the line? When do we decide not to conform to the norm? When do we break ranks with the majority? March to a different drumbeat?

The herd instinct is strong. We tend to follow the crowd because to resist or be different is costly and risky. We don't want to stand out or call attention to ourselves. Marches or demonstrations make us too visible. We may not need new clothes but the styles have changed. Who wants to be stared at because our clothes are out of style? A conversation may be flowing with ease and laughter, so why speak out for the victim or share another side of the issue and risk not being invited back? We like the security and acceptance of going with the flow.

At the same time, the poor continue to suffer and their plight worsens while many of us remain content with the status quo. "The poor you always have with you" is recalled. Without realizing it, we allow popular but inadequate interpretations of Scripture to sustain our apathy and indifference.

Those who are doing something constructive are risk-takers. Rosa Parks, the Black woman who refused to take a back seat on the bus in Montgomery, Alabama, was willing to risk being arrested and fined. She moved to risk-taking because conformity enabled an evil system to continue. Today she is honored as the one who ignited the great movement for civil rights that began in the 1950s.

Heroes and heroines of faith in the Scriptures all had one thing in common. They displayed courage at critical moments in their lives. They went against the stream, trusting that God would be with them. In responding to the cries of the hungry and oppressed, we often are called to act before all the evidence is in. We risk being wrong at times. That's part of the faithfulness involved in having compassion for people. No one said taking up the cross and being followers of Jesus would be risk-free.

● ● ●

I am not an exceptional man

Arnold, who has made his no-questions-asked peace with the world for $30,000 ($50,000 in today's money) a year, speaks to his ne'er-do-well brother, Murray, who has rebelled against the deceits of conventional society and cares about people passionately.

"I have long been aware, Murray . . . I have long been aware that you don't respect me much. I suppose there are a lot of brothers who don't get along.

Unfortunately for you, Murray, you want to be a hero. Maybe if a fella falls into a lake, you can jump in and save him; there's still that kind of stuff. But who gets opportunities like that in midtown Manhattan, with all that traffic? I am willing to deal with the available world and I do not choose to shake it up but to live with it. There's the people who spill things, and the people who get spilled on; I do not choose to notice the stains, Murray. I have a wife and two children, and business, like they say, is business. I am not an exceptional man, so it is possible for me to stay with things the way they are. I'm lucky, I'm gifted; I have a talent for surrender. I'm at peace. But you are cursed, and I like you, so it makes me sad, you don't have the gift; and I see the torture of it. All I can do is worry for you. But I will not worry for myself; you cannot convince me that I am one of the bad guys. I get up, I go, I lie a little, I peddle a little, I watch the rules, I talk the talk. We fellas have those offices high up there so we can catch the wind and go with it, however it blows. But, and I will not apologize for it, I take pride; I am the best possible Arnold Burns.

Herb Gardner

R evolt is Christian. But we must turn to it only in cases of necessity. When people are mutiny-minded, they sometimes insist that a case of necessity exists every time something opposes their own wishes. That is why it is good that revolt or mutiny always involves great outward risk—the judgment of God.

Christians always have maintained that a willingness to suffer is a practical test in these matters of whether we are rightly related to God. Christians also have considered absolutely sinful any mutiny based solely on personal desire.

Where God's orders are trodden underfoot and the right of others to live is threatened, the Christian must be willing to go the way of sacrifice, even if it involves revolt against illegal authority.

It is inappropriate for Christians to say that if the freedom of the church or of God's Word is not yet directly threatened, we ought not take suffering and strife upon

ourselves just for the sake of "secular matters." There are no
such things as "secular matters" for a Christian conscience.

Eivind Berggrav

We must have no illusions, we shall not walk on roses,
people will not throng to hear us and applaud, and we
shall not always be aware of divine protection. If we are to be
pilgrims for justice and peace, we must expect the desert.
When I give food to the hungry they call me a saint. When I
ask why they are hungry, they call me a Communist.

Dom Helder Camara

ROMANS 12:2
*Do not be conformed to this world but be trans-
formed by the renewal of your mind, that you
may prove what is the will of God, what is good
and acceptable and perfect.*

DANIEL 3:16–18
*Shadrach, Meshach, and Abednego answered the
king, "O Nebuchadnezzar, we have no need to
answer you in this matter. If it be so, our God
whom we serve is able to deliver us from the
burning fiery furnace; and he will deliver us out
of your hand, O king. But if not, be it known to
you, O king, that we will not serve your gods or
worship the golden image which you have set
up."*

REFLECTION • ACTION

1. Who has modeled courage for you in their response to human
suffering? What church or government leaders today demonstrate a willingness to risk for those who are considered the
nobodies in society?

2. Think through what the pressures and fears are that keep
you in "conformity to the world." What are some first steps you
could take to overcome those pressures, those fears?

3. Write a letter of appreciation to someone who has demonstrated courage in helping people. Keep in correspondence with someone who is on the front lines of opposition to injustice, pain, and oppression.

4. Read: *Through the Gospel with Dom Helder Camara,* by Dom Helder Camara, Orbis, 1986.

● ● ●

FROM TOO MUCH
TO ENOUGH

*If the world were merely seductive, that would be
easy. If it were merely challenging, that would be
no problem. But I arise in the morning, torn between
a desire to save the world and a desire to savor the
world. That makes it hard to plan the day!*

E. B. White

One of the most difficult areas for us to deal with, in our
response to hunger and poverty in the world, is our life-
style of relative greed and overconsumption. It is far easier to
give money, write letters advocating change, and attend Bible
studies on feeding the poor than to change ourselves and the
way we live. Our life-style is connected to how we move beyond
guilt and powerlessness.

Most of us in the First World eat too much, buy more than
we need, waste enormous amounts, consume more than our
share of natural resources, and spend too much on our own
security and pleasure. We constantly face the temptation to put
our security in material possessions. We are told over and over
again that happiness and status come from having rather than
being. It is a seductive world we live in.

Peter's first epistle says of the Christian, "You have been
born anew." Could it be that part of our conversion experience
is to a new understanding of economics? Can we continue to
support an economic system that is based on constantly ex-
panding production of goods and services? To make it work,
people must become dissatisfied or greedy so that they will buy
and consume more and more. This has all kinds of implications
for the environment, for our freedom from covetousness, and
for compassion for people on the bottom.

John Taylor, in his book *Enough is Enough,* introduces us
to the theology of enough. He suggests that the dreams by which
we live determine what economic systems we adopt. The law of
the Sabbath, the law of the tithe, the year of jubilee, the law of

the first fruits were laws of the Israelites, based on their dream of shalom for all people.

If we are to move beyond too much to enough, we will find that the issue of changing our life-style is important in our response to human suffering. Living more simply can be freedom for us, a freedom from insatiable appetites, as well as from the competition and success orientation that alienate us from one another. As Mary Schramm says, "Take one step at a time, but live with a renewed sense of intentionality toward patterns of living consistent with the providence of God and the vision of shalom for all God's people."

● ● ●

Getting in sync with the gospel

For me it started in Detroit, at a national camp directors' meeting, where John Schramm spoke. In a very gentle, "grace-filled" way he challenged me to look at my life. On the plane ride home I thought how freeing it would be to get my life more in sync with where the gospel invites me to be.

I came home thinking (and still believe) that there is no *one* place that a person must start in attempting to move to a more Christ-centered life-style. For me, the beginning place was salary. Being a parish pastor, I have the opportunity to discuss this with my "employers" each year. I first sit down with my wife, Mary, and we decide what we need in order to have "enough." The amount is not as important as the exercise in Christian stewardship we go through to arrive at our decision. It is good for our family, but also for the council and larger congregation.

The two primary challenges I face in attempting to live more simply are both close to home: my children and close relatives. The children cannot be isolated from a world that spends billions of dollars each year to convince them to consume. At ages 12 and 16, they provide some lively conversation for me as I attempt to challenge this "American way of life." Their values and mine continually are being shaped. I don't want them to take mine on as law, but I do want them to be aware of something besides the grossly consumer-oriented society in which they and I live.

Pastor Larry Peterson

● ● ●

Pastoral letter on U.S. economy

America's Roman Catholic bishops issued a ringing indictment of U. S. economic realities Thursday in approving their pastoral on the economy.

"Our faith calls us to measure this economy not only by what it produces, but also by how it touches human life and whether it protects or undermines the dignity of the human person," the letter said.

"This letter is a personal invitation to American Catholics to use the resources of our faith, the strength of our economy, and the opportunities of our democracy to shape a society which better protects the dignity and basic rights of our sisters and brothers in this land and around the world," the letter said.

The bishops outlined six major points:

"(1) Every economic decision and institution must be judged in light of whether it protects or undermines the dignity of human persons. (2) Human dignity can be realized and protected only in community. (3) All people have a right to participate in the economic life of society. (4) All members of society have a special obligation to the poor and vulnerable. (5) Human rights are the minimum conditions for life in community. (6) Society, as a whole, acting through public and private institutions, has the moral responsibility to enhance human dignity and protect human rights."

While recognizing that their statements would anger some, the bishops said, "In analyzing the economy, we reject ideological extremes, and start from the fact that ours is a 'mixed' economy, the product of a long history of reform and adjustment."

The letter also says, "The challenge of this pastoral letter is not merely to think differently, but also to act differently. A renewal of economic life depends on the conscious choices and commitments of individual believers who practice their faith in the world."

Martha Sawyer Allen

JEREMIAH 22:13–16

Woe to him who builds his house by unrighteousness, and his upper rooms by injustice; who makes his neighbor serve him for nothing, and does not give him his wages; who says, 'I will build myself a great house with spacious upper rooms,' paneling it with cedar, and painting it with vermilion. Do you think you are a king because you compete in cedar? Did not your father eat and drink and do justice and righteousness? Then it was well with him. He judged the cause of the poor and needy; then it was well. Is not this to know me? says the Lord.

REFLECTION · *ACTION*

1. John Taylor suggests that we join the cheerful revolution of resisting rampant consumerism. How can we do this cheerfully? What benefits would consuming less have for you? For your neighbor in need? For the environment?

2. What economic decisions did you make this past month? Measure them against the six major points of the Bishops' Pastoral Letter on the U.S. Economy. What dream forms our economics? Consider setting aside 1% of your income (over and above your weekly offering to your church) for causes that help the poor.

3. Read: *"To Celebrate—Reshaping Holidays and Rites of Passage,"* from Alternatives, Box 429, Ellenwood, GA 30049. Decide on new ways to celebrate Christmas and Easter that will be consistent with your values and concern for the poor. Write to Alternatives for ideas.

· · ·

FROM OWNERSHIP
TO STEWARDSHIP

The deterioration of the environment is an outward mirror of an inner condition—like inside, like outside. As we go through the checklist of environmental problems—from Chernobyl to Three Mile Island, from Love Canal to an agricultural landscape strewn with agrichemicals and uncontrolled soil erosion—one thing becomes increasingly clear: that we of the Judeo-Christian tradition have failed miserably to meet the assignment of the first work task given our forebears, "to care for the garden."

Wes Jackson

The metaphor of the "steward" carries important meaning for us in our search for a life-style appropriate to our calling as Christians. Douglas John Hall has suggested that stewardship is a way of conceiving the mission of the Christian movement in the post-Christian era. He contends that understanding stewardship is the key to our understanding the mission of seeking justice, peace and integrity of creation.

The movie *Oh God!* had profound insights related to stewardship. The manager of the market (played by John Denver) received a message from God (played by George Burns) to give to the world. But no one would listen, including religious people. The message God wanted to deliver was simple. "I'm here. I like you a lot. It can work (meaning the laws of nature and the universe which God set in order). And don't hurt one another." A good steward is one who believes that and lives accordingly.

The biblical understanding of stewardship implies accountability and participation. To move beyond guilt and powerlessness, we need to move from mastery, control, and ownership attitudes to an attitude of stewardship toward all of life. This means becoming caretakers of creation with a sense of identification and partnership, rather than domination and exploitation. To be a steward of creation is to embrace the world, to love the world as Christ did, and to be willing to sacrifice for the world rather than escape from the world.

The Shakertown Pledge was the outcome of a gathering of committed people seeking ways to respond to the cry for eco-justice. Notice its concern for accountability and participation.

● ● ●

THE SHAKERTOWN PLEDGE

R ecognizing that the earth and the fulness thereof is a gift from our gracious God, and that we are called to cherish, nurture, and provide loving stewardship for the earth's resources,

And recognizing that life itself is a gift, and a call to responsibility, joy, and celebration, I make the following declarations:

1. I declare myself to be a world citizen.

2. I commit myself to lead an ecologically sound life.

3. I commit myself to lead a life of creative simplicity and to share my personal wealth with the world's poor.

4. I commit myself to join with others in reshaping institutions in order to bring about a more just global society in which each person has full access to the needed resources for their physical, emotional, intellectual, and spiritual growth.

5. I commit myself to occupational accountability, and in so doing I will seek to avoid the creation of products which cause harm to others.

6. I affirm the gift of my body, and commit myself to its proper nourishment and physical well-being.

7. I commit myself to examine continually my relations with others and to attempt to relate honestly, morally, and lovingly to those around me.

8. I commit myself to personal renewal through prayer, meditation, and study.

9. I commit myself to responsible participation in a community of faith.

M other Earth is in jeopardy, caused by the anthropo-
centrism of religion, education, and science during the
past three centuries. A new beginning is required, centered on
the sacredness of the planet—its rainforests, oceans, soil, air,
and all the creatures of the Earth.

I believe that religion, science, and art must overcome
their antagonisms and work together to awaken the human
imagination and to heal the planet. The survival of the Earth
depends upon "reinventing our species" (Thomas Berry) so
that we live more harmoniously with nature. The new
cosmology that science, art, and mysticism unite to teach is
the ancient spiritual and ecological lesson: All things are
connected.

Matthew Fox

W e are asking an awesome question in this book: Will
there be food for tomorrow? The outcome of the world
food crisis, as well as the future course of American
agriculture, depends on whether the constant resource abuse
of the world can be stopped. This hoped-for reversal depends
most fundamentally on whether we humans are able to shift
from relating to the sustaining resources of the created world
as objects of exploitation to seeing resources as subjects of
God's order.

But is reversal possible? Where can we get help? The
ancient wisdom of the biblical tradition provides a firm basis
for building a needed ethic for our time. In this wisdom are
found fundamental insights for establishing the criteria
(value, attitude, measurement, policy) for a new agriculture,
an agriculture that can move us beyond the dominant
destructive trends of contemporary practice into a preferred
future.

C. Dean Freudenberger

LUKE 12:42
*And the Lord said, "Who then is the faithful and
wise steward, whom his master will set over his
household, to give them their portion of food at
the proper time? Blessed is that servant whom his
master when he comes will find so doing.*

PSALM 24:1

*The earth is the Lord's and the fullness thereof,
the world and they that dwell therein.*

REFLECTION • *ACTION*

1. What area of abuse to the created order (biotic community) have you become most concerned about? Why has it concerned you? What are you doing about it?

2. Which part of the Shakertown Pledge have you already taken? What would be the next step you need to take?

3. Do something concrete that will put you more in touch with nature and connect you with the importance of care of the earth. Learn from the American Indians about our relationship to the earth.

4. Read *The Steward: A Biblical Symbol Come of Age,* by Douglas John Hall, Friendship Press, 1985; and *Christian Ecology,* ed. Frederick W. Krueger, North American Conference on Christianity and Ecology, San Francisco, 1988.

● ● ●

FROM LOVING PEACE
TO PEACEMAKING

My conscience I have from God and cannot give to Caesar.

John Milton

It's a safe bet that a large majority of people favor peace over war. Despite what we favor, war is real and preparation for war is approved as a necessary deterrent. With so much of our national income going for defense spending, we are compelled to ask: Is this peacemaking?

There is a difference between peaceloving and peacemaking. One can be for peace but never really be a maker of peace. Our involvement in a largely defense economy is a seductive force in our society. We all seem to benefit either directly or indirectly from greater defense spending. It is difficult to resist something that works in our favor.

Each of us needs to think through our commitment to peacemaking and non-violence in both our work and leisure. How much have we been manipulated to fear the Soviets, our most recent "enemy," so that the weapon systems will go forward? As talks advance to reverse the arms race, what are we willing to do to make it happen? What are we willing to risk in our efforts of peacemaking?

● ● ●

The Demonstrator

She's a private person.
Not one to call attention to herself.
Never one to publicly criticize others.
Careful, gracious behavior
is her style.

Before acting, she asks,
"What would the neighbors think?"

She's a believing person.
A church-going,
Mission-supporting,
Bible-study leading
Seventy-seven-year-old person of faith.

Before acting, she asks,
"What would God think?"

She's a trusting person.
A government-supporting,
Law-abiding,
Voting,
Patriotic citizen.

Before acting, she asks,
"Is it democratic?"

She's a genteel person.
A wisp of a smile
Lays in a puff of soft white skin.
Two tender blue eyes peek out,
Open to faces around her.

Her attire belies her destination today:
    A ribbon-trimmed, wide-brimmed hat
    Accentuates white permed hair.
    A crisp white suit with blue trim
    Clothes her round frame.
    White-washed high heels
    Complete the look.
Is she going to a luncheon, a fashion show?
She's going to a parade.
She's going to *march* in a parade.

It's not much of a parade.
Twelve marchers . . .
If you count the baby
In the stroller.

At the head of the parade,
Behind the police escort
With his gaudy, blinking light,
Stands our unlikely demonstrator.

Shyly she greets her marching partner,
Then begins to converse:
   "My son went to war.
   When he came home, I said,
   'John, you're so thin!' "

"Mom," he replied,
"I've got my arms, my legs.
I can see and hear.
Just be glad I'm home."
Her partner nods, with tears.

Then—with strong resolve—
Our demonstrator states:
   "We who raise children
   Should *refuse* to send them off to war!"

The parade begins.
Forward it moves.
A private person takes a public stance.
A believing, trusting, genteel person
Marches in her high heels
Right down Main Street
Holding a banner high.
A banner with large red letters:
MOTHERS' PEACE MARCH!

Vivian Elaine Johnson

Where to start

Right after I left the weapons industry, I wrote an article about things that motivated me to leave. One of my friends who still worked at Lockheed took this article to work and put a routing slip on it and circulated it among the engineers I used to work with. Various ones wrote little comments on the back of the routing slip. When my friend received it back, after everybody had read and initialed it, he sent me the routing slip with the comments. Another friend there had written that "This ideology is correct indeed." In other words, he agreed with what I had written, but he thought it would have to be accepted by the whole world in order to have any meaningful effect. And then he ended with, "The question is where to start?" I think that if I were to answer that question, I would say that the place to start is with yourself, because you're responsible for what you're doing. When you begin to change your own life to live more according to these ideals that most, if not all, people hold, then it becomes very apparent what effect that one person can have.

In the Pacific Life Community with which I once worked in resisting injustices, we treated nonviolence as not only a tactic or a public witness, but also as a personal issue. We felt, and I still feel, that nonviolence starts first within—by rearranging the life-style to be less exploitive. Before we can overcome the Trident system that threatens global destruction, we must first overcome the Tridents within us that prevent us from relating to our brothers and sisters in this country and all over the world.

Robert Aldridge

D ear God, in the past—and still in our time—the church has given its blessing to the sword. Forgetting that the gates of hell shall never prevail against her, the church has developed "policies of survival" and become "security addicted."

We weep, O God, for a church so afraid of dying that it has compromised itself with the powers of this world. We weep for a church that sells its soul for "protection" and "peace" and the "freedom" to preach a heavenly gospel—so long as it does nothing to disturb the repressive, law-and-order society around it.

Ransom us, we pray. Ransom us so that we may at last, with you and your Spirit, enter Zion singing.

Roger Desir

MATTHEW 5:9
Blessed are the peacemakers, for they shall be called sons of God.

MICAH 6:8

He has showed you, O man, what is good; and
what does the Lord require of you but to do
justice, and to love kindness, and to walk humbly
with your God?

REFLECTION • *ACTION*

1. Can you think of times when your yes to God has meant saying no to some present accepted system or value in society? How has your no been borne out in your actions? What were the results?

2. National security is important to each nation. At what point does national security become an opponent to peacemaking, to the Christian faith?

3. Decide to do one special thing each month for the next year as a peacemaking effort. Ask your church to begin a peacemaking support group, and become one of its members. Remember, peace is in the making.

4. Read *The Arms Race Kills Even Without War* by Dorothee Soelle, Fortress, 1983.

• • •

FROM SILENT COEXISTENCE *TO ENCOUNTER*

O God, make me love justice, and seek equal job opportunity where I work, open housing in my apartment building or suburb, open membership in my club, better schools for all children in my city.

O God, make me hate wrong and speak out against it boldly, at parties, among my relatives, in my church board meetings, at work.

O God, keep me from being contentious, but make me care enough to contend for justice, against wrong, with humility.

Robert Raines

Almost all of us who have had our global consciousness raised run into friends, relatives, or neighbors who don't understand or don't appreciate our new perspective on various issues. It can be frustrating to explain to people what's happening to us, what we've learned, what we now view more critically, what new questions we've learned to ask, and what we have come to appreciate. Sometimes it seems best to remain silent, change the subject, or only touch the surface in our conversations about what we know will be controversial issues.

There is a time to be silent and a time to speak, a time to build and a time to tear down, a time to laugh and a time to cry—so says the wisdom writer of old. The important thing is to know which time it is. Most difficult is to find the courage to speak at the right time, knowing that to be silent is a betrayal of those who suffer.

For example, conversing with close friends and relatives about life-and-death issues that touch on politics and economics can be one of the most difficult aspects of our Christian witness. Yet such encounters are vitally important to our own integrity, our faithfulness to Christ, and our solidarity with the poor.

93

When we witness oppression, silent coexistence often is deadly. In these situations it is not our lives at stake, but the lives of millions in the Third World whose suffering continues because people like us, in the affluent nations, have not been willing to speak up.

We need to address this challenge imaginatively. In spite of intense differences, we can create accepting environments where significant issues facing Christians can be discussed and explored. As Jean Martensen says, "With God's help we can begin to transform our current arenas of tight-lipped coexistence into encounters that are both dynamic and faithful."

● ● ●

My brother and I disagree

My brother and I rarely agree on anything. The issues that polarize the American public tend to divide us too. Since our daughters were quite young when we moved to Geneva, Switzerland, I had not expected them to retain clear memories of the argumentative but fun-loving, good-natured uncle who helped us resettle in the United States in the summer of 1981. After seven years abroad with the Lutheran World Federation, I imagined our homecoming would find them as unprepared for him as they were.

Uncle John, our daughters quickly learned, was an unrepentant prankster. In public and in private, he left them laughing and redfaced. After a few short days together, however, they not only learned to accept this zany uncle from Phoenix but also to retaliate with sly jokes of their own. His unpredictable humor, I soon discovered, was not the source of their bewilderment.

What they found difficult to understand was how their uncle could be so different from their mother. Even harder to fathom was why these profound differences did not appear to threaten our relationship. Years later they still recall with wonder the night we lit the candles on the picnic table and argued—with considerable passion—for six straight hours about every topic imaginable: presidential politics, the international economy, the handling of hostages, immigration policies, causes of unemployment, environmental pollution, the role of religion in American life, the women's movement and its impact on us and our families, and more.

After years of virtually no contact, the list of concerns seemed inexhaustible. Too, the time abroad had furnished me with a global perspective on every subject that surfaced. It was as difficult for me to eliminate this consciousness from our discussion as it was for my brother to see its relevance to the case he was making. Yet, as divisive as these issues were, they never obliterated the unspoken rules of the debate. It was always equally important to both of us

- to affirm the other and to give each other space,
- to be aware of our feelings,
- to name and explore the real problems,
- to laugh at ourselves,
- to obtain both new information and new insights in the course of the exchange,
  - to empathize with each other,
  - to discover areas of mutual interest, and
  - to create new possibilities together.

Why? How did we come to rely on this unarticulated methodology? As children, I think, my brother and I gradually integrated this way of dealing with those who differed from us through a combination of historical demands, familial values, and exposure to the gospel of Jesus Christ.

Jean Martensen

I believe there is a time for patience and a time for impatience; a time for obedience and a time for disobedience—or a deeper obedience than that exacted by human laws and institutions. There is a time for continuity and a time for discontinuity. Ours are times—because of the unprecedented crises of Mother Earth, of our youth, of the spiritual vacuity of institutional Christianity in Europe, of the boredom that most worship instills in persons—for holy impatience, disobedience, and discontinuity.

Matthew Fox

Dear Mr. President:

I am a farmer, the son of a German immigrant who was so proud to become a citizen of the United States. During August 16–27 I traveled to Mexico, Honduras, and Nicaragua to get firsthand information about problems concerning world hunger. I am now very concerned that my tax dollars are being spent in military aid to Latin American governments that suppress the opportunity for the poor in society to develop. The people we had contact with did not want war. They wanted to be left alone to develop this society in their own way. This is the first time I have ever spoken out in this way. I have, in the past, felt our government was usually on the right track. After seeing and hearing firsthand from so many people, I feel I must not remain quiet.

John Everts

COLOSSIANS 4:6
Let your speech always be gracious, seasoned with salt, so that you may know how you ought to answer every one.

EXODUS 3:10
Come, I will send you to Pharaoh that you may bring forth my people, the sons of Israel, out of Egypt.

REFLECTION • *ACTION*

1. Reflect on the rules of the debate Jean Martensen uses in her encounters with relatives. Which are the more difficult for you? Why? How can these be applied to congregations as well as individuals?

2. What does it mean to be politicized? Can one be faithful to the gospel without getting involved in political issues? Who are the pharaohs in today's society that need to be addressed with the words "Let God's people go?"

3. Look for an opportunity where you can inject into the social conversation a positive word for the struggle of the oppressed.

Recommend an article or book to the person who seems open to an expanded view.

4. Become a member of Bread for the World, a Christian citizens' movement that informs people of legislative issues impacting hungry people. Address: 802 Rhode Island Ave. N.E., Washington, DC 20077.

● ● ●

FROM GOOD FRIDAY
TO EASTER

*When our preaching about the poor stops being
preaching and becomes our living on behalf of the
poor, then Easter is taken from the realm of myth
and becomes a powerful movement on the plane of
history where poverty brings an early death to so
many people. And when we, as Easter people, stand
up and say no to poverty, no to hunger, no to unemployment, we are robbing death of its power.
When we stand up on behalf of the poor and of
every person victimized by injustice, we are saying
the future is not closed. No lie can live forever. When
we take our hammers and saws and bend our backs
to transform shacks into affordable housing for people who never dreamed of living somewhere all their
own, we are testifying to the light that has come
into the world to enlighten every person. "No lie
can live forever."*

Kenneth Wheeler

D eath and resurrection have always been at the heart of the
Judeo-Christian faith. It predates Calvary and the empty
tomb. The idea of darkness and dawn, pain and healing, loss
and newness has been part of the creation's history from the
beginning. Out of chaos and darkness God created something
beautiful and good. We all were born into this world following
struggle and pain. Birthing always comes after struggle and ag-
ing.

Throughout these chapters we have been reminded that we
are people of hope who have been given energy for life. This
energy is born out of the experience of struggle, frustration, and
grief. The oppression and death of so many people overwhelms
us. In one way or another we identify with Rachel, who grieved
over the loss of her children.

99

JEREMIAH 31:15

A voice is heard in Ramah, lamentation and bitter weeping. Rachel is weeping for her children; she refuses to be comforted for her children because they are not.

We grieve over the millions who needlessly die of hunger. The environment is crying out in pain because of exploitation. Feelings of guilt, powerlessness, and fear, as well as anger, despair, and anguish, could lead us to look for an easier way. There is always the strong temptation to find an escape from Good Friday in order to come to Easter. Many churches have neglected or glorified Good Friday so that the greater emphasis could be placed on the resurrection. This is a mistake. No wonder there is a great deal of denial of reality or avoidance of grief over the injustice, oppression, and pain being experienced by so much of God's creation today. Making Christianity an otherworldly religion is an example of our denial of both Good Friday and Easter.

We are Easter people living in a Good Friday world. But there is no Easter until there is Good Friday. Not until we are willing to embrace the pain will we experience newness and power for healing. There is no hope if we quickly rush to the empty tomb without lingering at the cross. In our urge for order, security, and peace of mind, we may clamor for signs of hope that suggest the possibility of new life without grief and pain, without the cross.

Elie Wiesel has observed that the survivors of the Holocaust in Europe during World War II are precisely the ones who can yet believe in God, a God who suffers and cares. Other Jews who have not experienced such hurt doubt more easily. Perhaps it is no different for us Christians who crowd our churches on Easter without any experience of Good Friday. We are more prone to accept the status quo without criticism, protest, or grief.

The metaphor of Sarah is taken up by Isaiah when he announces to the exiles in Chapter 54 that things will be different. When it seems hopeless, a word of hope is given. When there seems to be no way out, the prophet announces that God will intervene. The barren one will have children.

ISAIAH 54:1

Sing O barren one, who did not bear; break forth into singing and cry aloud, you who have not been in travail! For the children of the desolate one will be more than the children of her that is married, says the Lord.

The biblical message of hope is one of surprise and newness that comes in the midst of despair and pain. It is a word that comes to those who have exhausted all other resources. This word of promise gives a fresh imagination of how things can be different. This hope enables us to believe in and work for a world of justice, equity, freedom, and shalom, because our God is free to act beyond the visible constructs of our present system.

The truths of Good Friday and Easter, once experienced, give us a new capacity to resist the forms of power that absolutize earthly systems, systems that favor some at the expense of others. We act in new ways, we carry on with a different vision, an enlightened imagination, even when there is little evidence that our dream will become a reality.

So we do not lose heart. We may be "struck down but not destroyed, perplexed but not driven to despair—always carrying in the body the death of Jesus, so that the life of Jesus may be manifested in our bodies" (2 Cor. 10). We continue to sing the doxology as our lives bear witness to this Easter hope.

> *Lead us from death to life, from falsehood to truth, from despair to hope, from fear to trust. Lead us from hate to love, from war to peace. Let peace fill our hearts. Let peace fill our world. Let peace fill our universe.*
> *Soli deo Gloria.*

Acknowledgments

Every effort has been made to trace the ownership of all material and to secure the permissions necessary to reprint these selections. Any error or oversight will be corrected in future printings if such omission is made known. Unless otherwise noted, all excerpts from personal correspondence refer to correspondence from the individual noted to George S. Johnson. We are grateful to the following individuals and publishers who have granted permission to reproduce their materials in *Beyond Guilt and Powerlessness* (listed in order of appearance):

Introduction: Personal correspondence from Tom Soeldner.

Chapter 1: Quote by Carter Heyward from Lutheran Human Relations Association of America 1988 Calendar; used by permission of LHRAA, 2703 N. Sherman Blvd., Milwaukee, WI 53210. Personal correspondence from Tom Soeldner. Quote from "The Biblical Concept of Justice" presented by Rolf Knierem to The ALC South Pacific District Convention, April 30—May 2, 1981.

Chapter 2: Quote from *Markings* by Dag Hammarskjold, translated by Leif Sjoberg and W. H. Auden; copyright © 1964 Alfred A. Knopf, Inc. and Faber and Faber Ltd. Sermon by Ernest T. Campbell. Quote from *The Cost of Discipleship* by Dietrich Bonhoeffer; copyright © 1959 SCM Press, Ltd; used by permission of SCM Press, Ltd. and Macmillan Publishing Company. Personal correspondence from Deborah Peters.

Chapter 3: Quotes from the article "Theological Education: Healing the Blind Beggar" by Walter Brueggemann in *The Christian Century*, February 5–12, 1986 copyright © 1986 The Christian Century; used by permission of The Christian Century Foundation. Quotes from the article "Yesterday's Victims Forgotten, Struggle Is on for Today's" by Elie Wiesel.

Chapter 4: Quote from "The Pathway of Peace: Father (Abuna Elias) Chacour," *SCAN* #521, Part 1, December 22, 1985. Quote by Dorothy Day from the *ELCA Hunger Program Newsletter*, Winter 1989.

Chapter 5: Quote from *Hopeful Imagination: Prophetic Voices in Exile* by Walter Brueggemann, copyright © 1986 Fortress Press. Article "We Sing Mary's Song" by Bonnie Jensen from *Word & World*, July 1987; used by permission of Bonnie Jensen and Luther Northwestern Theological Seminary, St. Paul, Minn.

Chapter 6: Personal correspondence from Don Christensen. Personal correspondence from Marilyn Borchardt. Article "Face to Face Encounters" from *Evangelism and the Poor* by Ana De Garcia and George S. Johnson, copyright © 1986 The American Lutheran Church.

Chapter 19: Quote by Robert Raines from *Creative Brooding*, copyright © 1966 Robert A. Raines. Article by Jean Martensen from *Peace Petitions*, Summer 1988. Quote from "Before Being Silenced by the Vatican" by Matthew Fox, editor, *Creation* magazine, P.O. Box 19216, Oakland, CA 94619. Personal correspondence from John H. Everts.

Chapter 20: Quote by Kenneth Wheeler from Lutheran Human Relations Association of America 1988 Calendar; used by permission of LHRAA, 2703 N. Sherman Blvd., Milwaukee, WI 53210.